The Delta Theorem

An Innovative Framework for Being Fully Alive and Truly Wealthy

The Delta Theorem

An Innovative Framework
for Being Fully Alive and Truly Wealthy

BRET MAGPIONG

Niche Pressworks

The Delta Theorem:
An Innovative Framework for Being Fully Alive and Truly Wealthy

ISBN-13: 978-1-952654-73-2 Paperback
978-1-952654-74-9 Hardback
978-1-952654-75-6 eBook

The information contained in this book is provided for educational and informational purposes only. The author and publisher are not engaged in rendering legal, financial, medical, or other professional advice. Any recommendations or suggestions in this book are not intended to replace or substitute for professional advice and services, and the reader should always seek the advice of a qualified professional before acting on any information in this book.

The author and publisher have made every effort to ensure the accuracy and completeness of the information in this book. However, they make no representations or warranties of any kind, express or implied, about the completeness, accuracy, reliability, suitability, or availability with respect to the information contained in this book. The author and publisher will not be liable for any loss or damage arising from or in connection with the use of or reliance on any information in this book.

The reader assumes full responsibility for any actions taken based on the information in this book. The author and publisher disclaim any liability, loss, or risk, personal or otherwise, incurred as a consequence, directly or indirectly, of the use and application of any of the contents of this book.

Any examples and case studies presented in this book are for illustrative purposes only and should not be considered as guarantees or predictions of any particular outcome. The results of any actions taken based on the information in this book will vary depending on a variety of factors, and the author and publisher do not make any representations or warranties as to any particular results or outcomes.

The content of this book may be updated, revised, or changed periodically without notice. The reader is responsible for reviewing the most current version of the book and ensuring that any actions taken are based on the most up-to-date information available.

By reading and using the information in this book, the reader acknowledges and agrees to the terms of this legal disclaimer.

For permission to reprint portions of this content or bulk purchases, contact info@ deltatheorem.com.

Published by Niche Pressworks; NichePressworks.com
Indianapolis, IN

The views expressed herein are solely those of the author and do not necessarily reflect the views of the publisher.

Dedication

To my daughter Brooke,
the Princess of the Great White Castle,
and the reason why I love being a GirlDad.
I hope this book will inspire you to live your life
with purpose, on purpose.

Acknowledgments

WELL, I GUESS this is the part where I roll up my sleeves and jump into the often overlooked but always important section of any book: the acknowledgments! It's the part where I publicly thank all the people who made this literary masterpiece possible. You know, those who didn't laugh (too hard) when I said I was writing a book, or who got me to stop watching SportsCenter when deadlines loomed, or who, most importantly, believed in me even when I doubted myself. Grab your favorite beverage and get ready for some good old-fashioned gratitude as we journey through the acknowledgments together.

First and foremost, to my wife, Leyla: Not only did you have to experience me being physically present but nowhere to be found mentally as I wrote during much of the last year, I thank you for being my first editor and my complete confidant. Not a chance this gets done without you. I love you.

Then there's my daughter, Brooke: Thank you for loving me in spite of myself. You inspire me to be fully alive.

To my dad, Earl Magpiong: Thank you for teaching me important Principles like "start slow and taper." That's what I did in the writing of this book.

To my mom, Irene Magpiong: Thank you for creating in me a tender heart. (And keep saving that space in heaven for me. I miss your hug.)

To Team Magpiong of Wellesley, Glen, Jane, TJ, Shannon, and Rosie — thank you for your listening ears and your wise advice.

To my brothers from other mothers, Brian Britt, John Allen, Jim Mudge, and Neal Ninteman: Thank you for being in my foxhole.

To the Cartel, Steve Heffernan, Mike Prock, Marc Daniel, and Jayda: Iron sharpens iron, but I have the tendency to be dull. Thank you for sharpening me.

To the DV Super Bowl crew, but especially Jim Inskeep: Thank you for encouraging me over all the years.

To my UM Boat Crews, but especially Don Voogd, Brett Hextall, Jamie Hurtubise, Paul Seidenkranz, Jim Brault, Richard Thompson, Brad Ritter, and everyone from Mentorship Alpha: Thank you for not voting me off any islands.

To all my work colleagues at Aspiriant, myCFO, The Bubble Factory, Saban Capital, and PriceWaterhouse: Thank you for putting up with my work shenanigans.

To my teams at Niche Pressworks (especially Nicole Gebhardt) and NGNG (especially Amber Vilhauer): Thank you for showing me how to get this book out of my head and into the marketplace.

To my editor, Melanie Hahn-Greene: Thank you for telling me I can actually write… and for cleaning up some of my poetic messes.

Without the love and support of my extended family and broad network of friends, I may never have experienced this journey. You are too many to name but know who you are. Thank you.

And finally, to the three-nutted peanut (aka three-in-one Trinity), the Father, the Son, and the Holy Ghost: I am nothing and know nothing without you in my life.

Contents

Introduction Getting off the Bus · · · 1

CHAPTER 1 It's the Framework, Stupid · · · 7
CHAPTER 2 Priorities Set the Course · · · 23
CHAPTER 3 Principles as Our Points of Leverage · · · 45
CHAPTER 4 Passion as a Flame · · · 63
CHAPTER 5 WHY Is the Point · · · 81
CHAPTER 6 Effort: The Accelerant · · · 97
CHAPTER 7 Failure Is an Option · · · 119
CHAPTER 8 Making a Difference · · · 137
CHAPTER 9 Just One Chisel Away · · · 153

Appendix Creating Rituals · · · 155
Thank You · · · 159
About the Author · · · 161
Endnotes · · · 163

INTRODUCTION

Getting off the Bus

IT WAS AFTER midnight on a Friday, and there I stood at a bus stop waiting for the L.A. Metro. I had just deplaned from the hour-long Southwest Airlines flight from San Francisco to Los Angeles.

Almost home.

A few months prior, I had taken an executive position with one of the country's largest and fastest-growing wealth advisory firms, Aspiriant. The role based me in The City (as I was learning San Franciscans liked to call it), miles away from my wife and daughter. They stayed in So Cal while I did the commute thing from L.A. to S.F. to L.A. every week.

It was far from ideal. Traveling through TSA twice a week never is, but we made it work.

The flight that night arrived late at LAX, and I didn't want my girls on the road picking me up. Too many "crazies" out at that time. (I was one of them.) Though I was tired, I thought, "Why not try the Metro?" I could certainly afford an Uber or a taxi — though, as I am the product of a very modest middle- to lower-middle-class upbringing, there was a time growing up when I couldn't.

Little did I know the kind of *Jerry Maguire*[1] opening-scene moment that ride would be for me. (If you haven't seen the opening scene, YouTube it. It's worth it.)

As the bus pulled up and I stepped on, I remembered looking around and wondering, "Am I on the wrong bus? Did this one come from the county jail, and I'm on it?" Yes, I got on at an official stop, but it soon became apparent that the sprinkling of fellow passengers was likely there because (1) they'd been on the wrong end of a DUI and lost their driver's license, a virtual death sentence for any car-loving resident of L.A. (we do love our cars), or (2) they could never have passed a driving test in the first place. One was even using the Metro as his own "motorhome" of sorts, all his earthly belongings in torn plastic trash bags snuggled close, like giant stuffed animals providing comfort and warmth as he slept.

It was certainly a far cry from where I'd been not all that long ago.

As an advisor to some of the wealthiest and most successful families in North America — several giants of industry, other giants of culture, many both — I often hobnobbed with those eligible for their own episode of *Lifestyles of the Rich and Famous.* The "Less Than One-Percenters." In one case, I even found myself flying private on the Boeing Business Jet, a full-sized 737, wholly customized with private bedrooms, bathrooms, kitchen, you name it. It was like flying Air Force One, only private.

Not gonna lie… it was sweet.

Yet, there I was on that bus. By choice. Late at night. Not feeling rich. Nor famous. More obscure, I would say, not unlike my fellow passengers, it seemed.

Maybe it was the environment on that bus, or perhaps it was the memory of that Boeing Business Jet, but as I watched the darkened shopfront windows pass, something surfaced inside that I still can't entirely explain. It was something having to do with the randomness of life. The ups and downs. The heartache. And the paradox.

"Here I am," I thought, "an advisor to many who have more money than anyone could ever dream of, yet I often hear them feeling like some on this bus (including me that night). Lonely. Isolated. Harried. Paranoid even." As I clutched my carry-on closer, I wondered where the feeling of life was in any of it.

I certainly didn't feel much aliveness on that bus. But I also didn't with many of my clients, who had so much wealth but often didn't feel wealthy. That was the paradox.

I remembered back to the summer after college graduation, just before launching into my career. That summer, I took a backpack, a sleeping bag, and all the money I could muster — which didn't amount to much, thus the backpack and sleeping bag — and ventured through Europe on a Eurail pass and hitchhiker's thumb.

It was a unique, eye-opening experience. A true "excellent adventure." And while I had many adventures during my few weeks there, I recalled one in particular at that moment on the bus: a stop at the Galleria dell'Accademia museum in the heart of Florence.

Why there?

As it turned out, inside the Galleria dell'Accademia, I found a hallway lined with several unfinished works of the great Renaissance artist Michelangelo. Appropriately known as *The Prisoners*, the works consisted of four blocks of marble with sculpted figures at various stages of completion. Some just a torso. Others with arms and heads as well. They all had an energy about them that felt like they were straining to escape their prisons of stone — struggling to come to life.

Maybe the best way to describe them is to have you picture yourself being dropped into a bed of wet cement. The cement has hardened, leaving half of your body buried and the other half not. The visible part of you is perfectly shaped and natural; the buried part feels trapped, struggling to break free.

I can only tell you it was mesmerizing.

But what was even more mesmerizing was that as my eyes gazed down to the end of the long hallway, they came upon one of the most amazing things I've ever seen: Michelangelo's *David*, a masterpiece like no other. Standing at a mind-blowing fourteen feet tall, *David* literally took my breath away. Every detail was carefully crafted and perfectly proportioned. He gazed out with nobility and greatness, his face filled with confidence and serenity.

It is magnificent, truly magnificent.

And while Michelangelo's legacy is filled with some of the greatest works in the history of art… works like the ceiling of the Sistine Chapel or the *Pietà*… *David* is quite possibly his most significant legacy piece of all.

After seeing it for myself, I certainly thought so.

Now, the reason the Galleria dell'Accademia always stuck with me was not just Michelangelo's works on display there. It was also *how* the works seemed to tell a story. A story not about pieces of art but about all of us. A story of struggle. Of transformation. Of perseverance.

A story, as I saw it, of coming alive.

We, too, start as blocks of raw material. Then, with the help of several of our own Michelangelos — be they parents, teachers, coaches, or friends — there's a chipping away until a uniqueness starts to take shape. Finer details surface. We struggle for freedom and independence until, ultimately, we unveil our glory and splendor for all the world to experience.

I don't think I'm being overly dramatic here. That's what I saw in that layout, starting with *The Prisoners* and ending with *David.*

Unfortunately, though, reality tells a much different story.

The marble we're made from? It often has flaws. The chipping? Uneven. Our uniqueness? Hidden. And even when we are unveiled, we don't feel like a masterpiece.

That was certainly the reality I experienced with many of my clients. It was the reality I saw on the bus. And it was a reality I felt myself.

Back on that bus, my mind started spinning, and I began to think.

"There has to be more to all this. More to the magnificence I felt at the foot of the *David.* Maybe bringing marble to life for Michelangelo wasn't just about his sculpting skills. Maybe there was something in his tools as well. Maybe there are hammers and chisels we can use on our own lives and the lives of others that can bring life. Real life."

I began to feel like I was onto something.

"And maybe, just maybe, once we lived fully alive, we would understand what it means to be wealthy. Truly wealthy. And not just financially, but relationally, physically, spiritually, mentally, and with our time."

Reaching my stop and getting off the bus that Friday night, I had no idea how my life was about to change, but it was. I was ending my journey on the bus, but starting a new journey, a journey of exploration, of experimentation, of discovery. A journey that ultimately led to the Delta Theorem... and the book featuring it, which you now hold in your hands.

CHAPTER 1

It's the Framework, Stupid

*"Don't ask yourself what the world needs.
Ask yourself what makes you come alive
and go do that. Because what the world needs
is people who have come alive."*

— Howard Thurman

LIFE IS TOUGH
IT'S EVEN TOUGHER
IF YOU'RE STUPID

THAT WAS THE bumper sticker on the tailgate of the old red Chevy Silverado I came across during my morning exercise regimen.

For at least the past 25 years, I have made it a ritual to rise early, do a few "first thing in the morning" activities, and then exercise by hitting the streets. Start strong. Stack actions. Get my day off right.

For me, the regimen works.

I'm usually very observant during my workouts, but I don't recall having ever seen that bumper sticker before. On this morning, it stopped me dead in my tracks. There was something about it that captured me.

Though very similar to a more cynical bumper sticker — "Life is tough, then you die" — this one was strikingly different. More informative. Almost hopeful, in a strange kind of way.

"What is it about that word 'stupid' that seems so crass and insensitive, yet so alluring?" I wondered. Little did I know that question would ultimately contribute to developing the Delta Theorem.

But first, a little about how I got there.

THAT DREADED FEELING

When it comes to memorable lines from movies, I can be something of a cinema nerd — the kind who can obnoxiously come up with some random movie quote for almost any situation. (It may be more of a guy thing; I don't seem to run across too many women who do it.)

Perhaps you know the type:

> You're with them at dinner when the check comes, and they blurt out, "Show me the money!" (Cuba Gooding, Jr. in *Jerry Maguire.*)
>
> Or, maybe you're thinking about retirement and ask them for a bit of advice whereby they rattle off, "Just

> when I thought I was out, they pull me back in!" (Al Pacino in *The Godfather: Part III*[2]).

> Or you're in unfamiliar surroundings, and they playfully say, "Toto, I've a feeling we're not in Kansas anymore" (Judy Garland in *The Wizard of Oz*[3]).

Yep, I am ***that*** guy, and coming across that bumper sticker was no exception.

It reminded me of a scene from the 2002 movie, *The Emperor's Club*, in which Professor William Hundert, skillfully played by the actor Kevin Kline, is a teacher of the classics at a stuffy East Coast prep school. Hundert strongly believes in shaping his students by using a very principled approach in his instruction.

Prim. Proper. High etiquette.

His methods are tested when a senator's son and cocky new student, Sedgewick Bell, enters the picture. During an impromptu quizzing in front of the entire class, Bell's condescension and arrogance are in full throttle, prompting Hundert to say in exasperation:

> "Mr. Bell, a word of warning. As the great wit Aristophanes once wrote — roughly translated — youth ages, immaturity is outgrown, ignorance can be educated, and drunkenness sobered. But STUPID lasts forever."[4]

The disparagement cuts into Bell like a knife to the gut. It's written all over his face. Insecurity. Humiliation. Shame. It's a deep wound that feels all too familiar and is something we all fear.

To feel stupid.

To be called stupid.

To do something stupid.

NEGATIVITY BIAS

Many studies have explored the power that emotional cuts and insults have on us. We humans have a universal tendency known as negativity bias, which is the habit of allowing negative emotions to affect us more strongly than positive ones. Researchers have discovered that receiving and internalizing negative comments increases stress, anxiety, frustration, and worry[5].

In other words, being stupid does indeed make life tougher. That was the pull I felt from that bumper sticker — the painful truth behind what it had to say.

EXPERIENCING THUNDERDOME

That scene brings to mind a very similar incident from my early schooling that lingers to this day. No, I didn't attend an east coast prep school, nor was I schooled in the classics, but I did do eight years of Catholic elementary school. That was classic enough.

While many "survivors" of Catholic school are quick to give accounts of the knuckle-cracking nuns, my memory recalls the math competitions that used to take place. No matter the grade level, the teachers followed a standard operating procedure: They created two parallel lines of students from the back of the room to the chalkboard up front.

Upon reaching the board, a student stood in the full spotlight with nowhere to hide. The teacher would rattle off a math problem, and the two students at the board would race to determine who would first write the correct answer. "Win," and you tally a point for your team while proudly running to the back of the line to do it again; "lose," and you feel stupid-shamed.

It was like Thunderdome in the Mad Max series.[6] Two students enter, one student leaves. (Remember what I said about being *that* movie guy???)

In this time-honored tradition of meaningless math competitions, I tended to excel. Often, I would look across at the competition and see several of my adversaries peering over, calculating down our line to see who they would face. Some would switch places with the unsuspecting teammate in front or behind to avoid going head-to-head with me.

Truth be told, I did the same with others, too.

On one particular day, I was at the board facing one of the "weaker" opponents when something seemingly improbable happened. The teacher gave the problem, and I… faltered. Badly. No matter how many times I posted an answer — and I recall the number being several — the answer was wrong. And with each failed attempt, I could feel my teammates' disbelief and groans and the opposition's disbelief and delight.

And then it happened.

After what seemed like an eternity, my opponent finally posted their first answer, a correct one. Winner, winner, chicken dinner!!! And there I was, left to carry the mental "scarlet letter" of the moment to the end of the line… only this letter was an "S" for stupid.

Stupid does seem to last forever — or at the very least, a long, long time. Cracked knuckles haven't stuck in my memory, but the shame of that big, heavy "S" certainly has.

WHY START WITH "STUPID"?

I'll be honest. In starting a book about coming alive, focusing first on a word with synonyms like "moron," "idiot," "half-wit," "pea brain," and "fool," all of which form an endless Hall of Shame list of insults, is, well, probably pretty stupid. It certainly risks offending or embarrassing you or at least making you feel awkward right about now. And it makes me look very politically incorrect. But stick with me because all of that is practically the point.

It certainly doesn't take a genius to understand that life is tough. Just live a little, and you experience it. Rents. Mortgages. Layoffs. Pandemics. Even kids. (Apologies to my daughter if she's reading this!)

It certainly doesn't take a genius to understand that life is tough. Just live a little, and you experience it.

And that's nothing in comparison to the significant losses that many face. Deaths. Depressions. Bankruptcies even. It makes looking for ways to an easy life practically an occupation, and it's maybe even why you picked up this book in the first place. Quick fix. Easy hack.

But that's not the way life works.

Life isn't about finding an easy way out. It's about learning to cope with the challenges that come your way and making the most of every situation. You have to accept that life will always be full of hardships, but it doesn't mean you can't still find joy in it. Rather than seeking quick fixes, focus on developing skills that will help you in the long run.

Over the years, I've thought a lot about that big S and what it means. And all that thinking started to build into a framework that I could think of as "the opposite of S."

THE OPPOSITE OF "S"

One cornerstone was the realization that while many people think smart is the opposite of stupid, it isn't. Wisdom is the opposite of stupid. Smart implies quick-witted intelligence regardless of experience or knowledge. Wisdom, on the other hand, includes experience, knowledge, and good judgment.

For instance:

- It's smart to stop smoking cigarettes; it's wise to have never started in the first place.
- It's smart to have goals; it's wise to hire a coach to hold you to them.
- It's smart to have started this book; it's wise to finish it. (And, I might add, it's stupid to quit now.)

What, then, can we do to avoid making life tougher than it already is? How can we avoid being a fool? How can we stop making life tougher by being stupid?

We can be wise, and if we are smart, we will learn to be wise as quickly as possible.

Nowhere is using wisdom more important than in managing our lives. And maybe nowhere is it more important than our view of wealth.

REVISITING THE FRAMEWORK FOR VIEWING WEALTH

While I've been a financial advisor throughout my career, my real purpose was never about managing money in the traditional sense. It was about aligning my clients' capital with everything else in their lives to create true wealth beyond the money.

Don't get me wrong. Money is important, but it isn't the end goal. The end goal is living with purpose, on purpose. That's when we are truly wealthy.

And that's where the Delta Theorem comes in.

The Delta Theorem is a foolproof framework developed to help anyone come alive with purpose, on purpose. It was what I consciously began developing after getting off that city bus.

It's not a quick fix or hack. It's a process based on smarts and wisdom. By following it, we create value by being difference-makers in our personal lives, our business lives, and our community lives.

Why did I need to develop an entirely new framework?

As someone who has spent his entire 35-plus-year career in wealth advisory roles, I was troubled that traditional wealth management used a one-size-fits-all approach, where all clients, regardless of their unique fears, concerns, values, priorities, and dreams, go through a standard process involving risk questionnaires and net worth statements. This standard approach often results in the same cookie-cutter advice and recommendations, focusing almost exclusively on financial wealth.

What I found, though, is that people are seeking satisfaction across various dimensions of life, not just the financial. And that includes me. They wonder what their wealth is doing to their kids. Or how their wealth might allow them more time to build community. Or how their wealth might build a transcendent legacy.

They want to balance material possessions with a sense of purpose and fulfillment.

I didn't want to keep operating in this old, outdated framework. Instead, I believe we need something new — something that brings the right elements together in a way that works for the whole person, not just his or her money.

The first thing was to start thinking more deeply about wealth and how to define it better. And not just any wealth, but the kind of wealth we're all ultimately after: True wealth, the kind that brings about that sense of purpose and fulfillment.

True Wealth Follows a Process

Thinking deeply about true wealth, I started to realize it was actually much less complicated than I initially thought.

Becoming truly wealthy starts by first experiencing greater aliveness. This aliveness brings awareness to what lies deep within that allows us to uncover skills and talents and make a positive difference in ourselves, our communities, and the environments we find ourselves in. Once we make a positive difference in the world, we cultivate deeper connections and have an impact, thus creating value with all that we do. And where we add value, we are more likely to generate wealth — only this is the kind of wealth that integrates the financial with the mental, spiritual, relational, physical, and temporal dimensions of life.

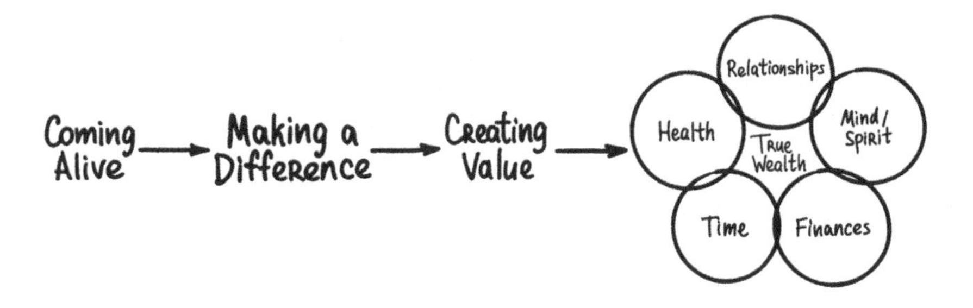

This underlying framework became the power behind the Delta Theorem.

THE DELTA THEOREM: THE TOOL FOR COMING ALIVE

I know. I know. The Delta Theorem. Sounds a little intimidating, doesn't it? It's not. Once you understand what it is, you'll be surprised by its simplicity.

Let me explain…

It's Not About Math

First off, while I put the Theorem in the form of a mathematical equation, it's not actually an equation at all. It's a framework laying out a process to come alive by breaking the process into variables to make it easy to see how things work together.

Unlike an equation, a framework doesn't have an absolute right or wrong answer. A framework makes room for necessary and appropriate adjustments along the way. If you don't like the results, you get the first time, you can examine the inputs you plug in and change something where you need to.

And second, I put it in the form of an equation to make it easier to remember. Plain and simple. Not much more than that.

So, if you're saying to yourself, "But I was terrible at math and have always hated it," you can relax. You don't need to be an Einstein or anything even close to understand the Delta Theorem and apply it. You don't have to do math at all.

The Delta Framework

All right, now that I've explained that part, here is the Delta Theorem:

$$\frac{\alpha}{p^3} \times \varepsilon f^2 = \Delta$$

Where α = powerful WHY
p^3 = Priorities · Principles · Passion
ε = Effort
f = Failure
Δ = Difference/Change/Impact

When spoken, it sounds like this: "Alpha over P-cubed by E, F-squared equals Delta." (As you say it a few times, you'll see what I mean by being easy to remember.)

One of the first things you may notice is that, like equations, the Theorem is made up of several variables. But, as I said, in the Delta Theorem, the variables operate differently. You are in charge of deciding what to plug in for each variable because you are unique. And so are your inputs. You use the framework to understand how your variables work together to create your own "right" answer — not "the only" correct answer.

Following are brief rundowns for each of the variables:

Alpha (α)

I chose the Greek letter "alpha" for a reason: as the first letter in the Greek alphabet, it's meant to signify your primary purpose, your "most important thing," your reason for being.

In *The Will to Meaning*, holocaust survivor Viktor Frankl says that the desire to find and create meaning is the primary motivating force in one's life. It's the one thing a person is willing to live and die for.[7]

In the Theorem, Alpha (α) is that motivating force.

Priorities | Principles | Passion (ρ^3)

In construction, as in life, firm foundations support buildings and structures, distributing loads evenly and preventing shifts that might occur over time. For Alpha to maintain its sturdiness, it must be built on a solid foundation. In the Theorem, that foundation is the integration of your Priorities, Principles, and Passion (ρ^3).

We'll look more at these in later chapters.

Effort (ε)

No movement happens without Effort. Effort, then, is the energy to do something, exert force, and take action. It's what happens when you show up, engage, and do work. Purpose, Priorities, Principles, and Passion are only activated by putting in the Effort.

Failure (f^2)

Most see failure as a negative. In math, when you square a negative, you get a positive. Similarly, when you square a failure by learning from it, you transform that negative into a positive.

Failure, then, is the opportunity to learn from our mistakes.

Delta (Δ)

In the world of mathematics, delta (Δ) is not just another Greek letter variable. It plays highly important roles in both physics and calculus. For our purposes, the main thing to remember is that Delta is what results from the interaction of all the other variables in the framework. You put yourself in the best position to make a difference and create true wealth in all five areas — financial, social/relational, mental/

spiritual, physical, and temporal — the wealth that's so difficult to attain without all the right elements in place.

There is No Formula to Real Life

As you can see, the variables of the Theorem are based on common sense and even intuition. But please remember that the Delta Theorem isn't a one-size-fits-all formula.

> There is no perfect formula for living that works for every person. Every life is unique. You are no exception.

There is no perfect formula for living that works for every person. Every life is unique. You are no exception. So, while the Theorem takes the shape of an equation, it's more like a recipe than an absolute formula. It's a framework for putting together ingredients — variables — to achieve an outcome. The variables you plug into your framework will look nothing like mine or anyone else's around you — and neither will the results.

As you explore the following chapters, I know you will gain insight about yourself that can lead to better wisdom throughout the more extensive journey of life. You may even realize (as I did) that you're holding onto some stupid assumptions that keep you from achieving what you want — making an actual difference where it will count most, not only for others but also for you.

The Delta Theorem is created especially for that reason — to take us out of the old, tired, haphazard (and yes, potentially stupid) formulas we've been trying to operate in and to use a smart framework instead. With it, we can gain wisdom that will continue to grow and further enrich our lives.

And while the Theorem ultimately puts you in a position to experience true wealth, this is not a get-rich, wealth management book. Instead, it's a book that lays out a journey to come alive.

Let's start the journey by taking an in-depth look at Priorities.

SHOW UP | ENGAGE | DO THE WORK

Take some time to answer the following:

1. What has been your experience with learning new things? Do you often have to work hard to understand new concepts, or do they come quickly to you?

2. How do you approach problem-solving and decision-making? Do you tend to rely on your instincts, or do you take a more analytical approach?

3. How do you handle challenges or setbacks? Do you see them as opportunities to learn and grow, or do they discourage you?

4. Do you enjoy learning new things and exploring new ideas, or do you prefer to stick with what you already know?

5. How do you view your intelligence and wisdom? Do you feel confident in your ability to learn and grow or feel limited in some way?

CHAPTER 2

Priorities Set the Course

"Time has a wonderful way of showing us what really matters."
— Margaret Peters

FOR MUCH OF my daughter's early education, I pulled my car into her school's parking lot to drop her off for the day. It started when she was in kindergarten and continued almost every school day until she learned to drive.

It was Brooke and Daddy's Weekday Excellent Adventure, and the ritual always looked the same:

- Load into the car after a mad dash out the door… with her buckled in the back seat, me in the front;
- Crank up Rare Earth's *I Just Want to Celebrate*, me bellowing out how I want to celebrate another day of livin',

and she playing drum solos and occasional air guitar in my rearview mirror;

- Drive past Dave, the perpetually smiling crossing guard, greet him with a quick toot of the horn, and shout out, "Hey Dave, have a great day!";
- Park in the South Bay Junior Academy parking lot;
- Walk, holding her hand, from car to classroom;
- Say goodbye with my special "tap-to-heart/tap-to-lips/kiss-to-her" bye-bye.

On this one particular morning, something changed.

As we got out of the car, Brooke had an odd look on her face, which I noticed but couldn't fully make out. We had both seen several of her peers — some carrying backpacks and others raising the flag — when we pulled in, but she must have noticed that they saw her too because when I went to grasp her hand as I always did, she looked at me with her second-grader eyes and said sheepishly, "Daddy, can we not hold hands?"

Ah, now I understand the look, I thought. It was a look of confused apprehension mixed with coming of age. I knew what she was asking. My girl wanted to grow up. She felt peer pressure but still, I sensed, didn't want to totally let go.

Don't we all?

Instead of playfully acting like I was hurt — or worse yet, actually **being** hurt — I matter-of-factly responded, "Sure, honey, we don't have to hold hands." Then, after a few steps, sensing she didn't want to completely give up being daddy's little girl, I leaned close to her ear and whispered, "But can we sometimes?"

She looked at me, smiled, and nodded a sweet Yes.

KNOWING WHAT'S IMPORTANT

Priorities. We all have them. The life commitments that genuinely matter to us. Commitments we focus on first above all else. Commitments to push our boundaries and pursue our hearts.

The Merriam-Webster dictionary defines commitment as a pledge to do something in the future[8]. That's precisely what a Priority is, a pledge to do something in the future. But rather than a pledge with someone else, it is a pledge with ourselves. We envision a future we want, and it becomes our Priority to pursue it.

> A Priority is a pledge with ourselves to do something in the future.

In that school parking lot, Brooke's Priority was pursuing friendships. Mine was her. It was a lesson I'll never forget and has stayed with me ever since.

An Endless List of What Matters

In our world of fast-moving narratives, instant gratification, hustle culture, and FOMO (Fear Of Missing Out), the list of priorities can feel endless. Often, we can feel stress deciding what should and shouldn't matter, what should and shouldn't be important. Friendship. Career. Grades. Money. Fame. Everything can seem like a Priority.

Seldom do we look within to sort them out.

For instance, a popular model of sorting priorities uses importance and urgency to organize actions. Known as the Eisenhower Method, the method originated with a quote from former U.S. President Dwight Eisenhower, in which he said, "I have two kinds of problems, the urgent and the important. The urgent are not important, and the important are never urgent."[9]

Using the Eisenhower Method, you evaluate actions using the criteria important/unimportant and urgent/not urgent, and place them in quadrants as follows:

1. Important/Urgent tasks are done immediately.
2. Important/Not Urgent tasks get assigned a later date.
3. Unimportant/Urgent tasks are delegated.
4. Unimportant/Not Urgent tasks are dropped.

The problem with the Eisenhower Method is that everything tends to end up in the Important/Urgent quadrant, and we end up with a matrix that looks like what former BlackRock hedge fund Managing Director, now Solopreneur and founder of *RadReads*, Khe Hy, has so accurately illustrated on the right[10].

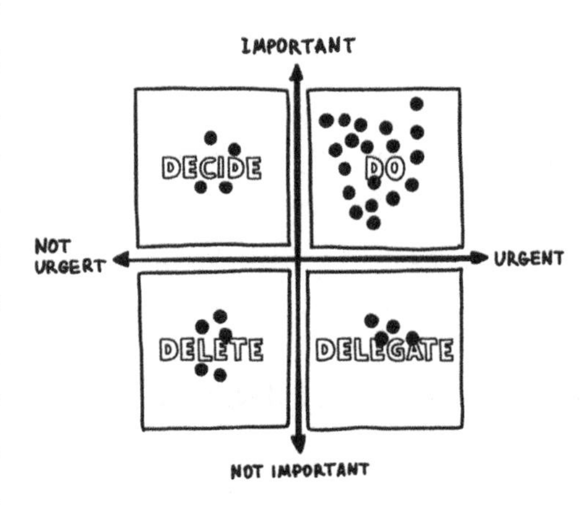

That's why it's essential to narrow down your priorities by asking yourself questions like:

- Where do I want to give my time?
- How do I want to spend my treasure?
- On what do I want to use my talents?

And when you look deep enough, you frequently uncover what matters most by discovering what you value.

Take my client, Erin, for example.

When Erin inherited a significant sum of capital, I worked with her to discover what was important regarding her wealth. "What matters when you think of the money you have?" I asked her.

Erin's response surprised me.

While I thought she might mention great causes to support or buildings to construct and name, Erin, instead, viewed the capital as a personal responsibility. It was a commitment to preserve the memory of her grandfather, the man who had put in all the hard work and sacrifice to earn it. To do otherwise, she said, "would be like walking on his grave."

From there, we developed strategies to honor that commitment.

Or take another client, Doug.

For many years, Doug had abused his body with drugs and alcohol. Eventually, he hit the proverbial rock bottom, slamming into it when he was unceremoniously ushered from a job he liked and was good at. His drinking had done him in. He knew he needed to get his act together because if he didn't, he would die. So, he started attending Alcoholics Anonymous to restore his health.

After five years of sobriety, Doug still values his health, though now it's through continuous improvement of his 5K's and 10K's, mentally, physically, and emotionally. We work on tactics together.

Both Erin and Doug were crystal clear on what they valued. For Erin, it was a grandfather's legacy. For Doug, it was his life.

PRIORITIES VS. PRIORITIZING

Many of us get confused and think that Priorities and prioritizing are the same. They're not. Distinguishing between the two is essential.

Prioritizing is the process of ranking actions to be taken to complete a project or reach a goal. They're activities in the day-to-day get-it-done mode that you sort in order of importance. They're written out on To-Do lists and organized by what's to be done first, sometimes using a system like the Eisenhower Method we previously discussed.

On the other hand, Priorities are life commitments that genuinely matter to you.

Like true north on a compass, Priorities orient you toward the life you want to live. They don't get entered neatly into a block of time on your calendar; they are the object of your calendar. You use them as yardsticks to measure your decisions, helping you stay on track and make the most of your time. When you start to feel overwhelmed or off-track, taking a step back to check in with your Priorities can give you clarity and direction.

Unfortunately, you might mistakenly start thinking the activities themselves are Priorities. They're not, at least not the way I mean Priorities in The Delta Theorem. An activity is not a Priority. *The aim is the Priority.*

For instance, you might prioritize going to the gym, but your Priority is health when you make having the energy for extended longevity a key focus of your life. (That was the case for Doug.) Similarly, you prioritize showing up to the office by 9 a.m., but your Priority is your career when you explore a true calling. Or maybe you prioritize going to church, but your Priority is spirituality when you search out the purpose of life.

I like to think of it as the difference between verbs and nouns. Verbs are actions, such as going to the gym; nouns are the subjects of those actions, such as "health."

You prioritize your actions; you make the subjects of your life your Priorities.

NARROWING IT DOWN

Let's face it, saying yes to too many things can be as painful as saying no. We can overcommit and underdeliver. Similarly, saying that something is not a Priority is not the same as saying it will not be pursued. Instead, it's saying it will be pursued less than something else. That's why it's essential to narrow your Priorities to a few higher-level commitments based on what matters most.

Below is a list of some of the most common higher-level commitments most of us pursue. They're not listed in any order but sum up most of the higher-level commitments we are bound to make.

- Work/Career
- Extended Family
- Friendships
- Spirituality/Religion
- Children
- Health/Fitness
- Possessions
- Volunteering/Altruism/Community
- Recreation/Fun
- Personal Responsibility
- Social Standing
- Hobbies/Sports
- Personal Growth/Education
- Money/Wealth
- Partner/Spousal Relationship

Exploring these higher-level commitments can be very helpful as you narrow down your Priorities.

And as you're deciding what's most important, here's another thing to keep in mind: there's a dark side to Priorities, and some Priorities are not beneficial to pursue.

THE DARK SIDE OF PRIORITIES

Over and over again, we find reminders that life is more a team sport than an individual one. We are made to be in relationship. What's good for the hive is good for the bee.

But what's good for the bee is not always good for the hive. A fixation on self alone typically leads to trouble. As German philosopher Friedrich Nietzsche said, "The worst enemy you can meet will always be yourself."[11]

This is never more evident than when making ourselves the primary focus of what's important. When we do, it usually happens in the following ways:

Self-Centeredness

I love this quote from Ryan Holiday: "We must accept that some people — for whatever reason — are destined to fill that undesirable quota of awfulness that the natural order seems to demand."[12]

Most often, this quota is filled with those who are self-centered.

The self-centered are easy to spot. They're the ones who are vain and full of themselves. They show an excessive need for admiration and lack empathy and consideration for other people. They're cocky, manipulative, selfish, patronizing, and demanding. They tend to turn any blame away from themselves and onto others.

They are their own top Priority. And, in most cases, their *only* Priority.

It should be easy to see why making self-centeredness a Priority is problematic. When you do, no one wants to be around you.

Nothing more needs to be said.

Self-Protectiveness

All of us experience distressing — even traumatic — events that cause us to cope by burying or suppressing our emotions, putting them aside where we're only partly conscious of them.

This is only a short-term solution, though.

If you do it over time, you start projecting danger into everything. You begin to think situations or people are fundamentally dangerous and to be approached with extreme caution, if at all.

You become so guarded that self-protection is the top Priority in your life.

To some extent, you must protect yourself. But when you are so self-protective that you become a shut-in, you lose many of the joys of life. Rather than no one wanting to be with you, as is the case in self-centeredness, you want to avoid being with others, which can lead to feelings of isolation, loneliness, and even paranoia.

Self-Destructiveness

At some point, we've all done something self-destructive. It's usually not on purpose and doesn't necessarily characterize us. It can appear in obvious behaviors, such as overusing alcohol, or in less obvious ones, such as wallowing in self-pity. But at its core, self-destruction can come from anything that causes self-harm.

Knowing that their actions are self-destructive, many people choose to do them anyway. The urge is too strong to control. These are the people who have made self-destructive behavior a Priority.

My alcohol-addicted client, Doug, certainly operated in this way, and so do many others who face addictions of any kind. And again, it's not too difficult to point out the problems this behavior creates.

The purpose here is to acknowledge that sometimes we prioritize self, but it's often to our detriment. Awareness, then, is essential.

(As a coach, it is beyond my training and expertise to address many of the issues underlying these darker Priorities. If or when I encounter any of them, I immediately refer a counselor or therapist qualified to handle these challenging issues. If you're dealing with any of the previously mentioned issues, I suggest you find help from a professional qualified to help you work through your situation while also putting the rest of this book into practice.)

IMPACT OF LIFE EVENTS AND ERAS

Unlike some other elements in the Delta Theorem, your Priorities frequently change in response to two types of occurrences: Life Events and Eras.

Life Events

Moments that change everything — things like pregnancies, deaths, marriages, divorces, job losses, or promotions, to name a few — often arrive unannounced. Priorities often shift with the expected and unexpected life events you experience.

A health scare or diagnosis can make your physical state a top Priority. An economic downturn can make wealth a top Priority. Losing a loved one can make friendships or spirituality a top Priority.

Erin experienced receiving an inheritance as a significant life event, while for Doug, it was losing a job. They both reflected on those events and set or reset their Priorities to guide their futures accordingly.

When I started working with another client, Tim, he and his wife had just moved into a new apartment. He was progressing in his career with a digital marketing company, and she was working on becoming an influencer in the world of interior design. He felt like they were both focused on their respective careers as Priorities.

Then it happened. Tim's wife got pregnant with their first child, and everything changed.

The yoga classes became Lamaze classes. The home office became a nursery. The money earmarked for vacations became an education fund, all with the onset of a single but significant life event.

Eras

Priorities also change with different eras. For instance, consider the following:

In our late teens, we are likely finding our way into adulthood. We may be starting our first real job or getting our first apartment.

For me, it was going to college as something of a double major. Business Administration. And rugby. (A triple major if you considered co-eds.) I was also a founding father of the newest fraternity at Cal Poly, San Luis Obispo. ITK – I Tappa Kegga. While not a Bluto or Flounder from *Animal House*[13], it's safe to say my late-teens era was a mixture of cramming for tests, avoiding getting killed on the rugby pitch, and partying during whatever time was left over.

In our 20s, we may be focused on building our careers and finding our life's work. We may also be exploring relationships and starting families.

In our 30s, we may work hard to establish our social standing while raising young children and juggling work and family responsibilities.

In our 40s, we may be in the prime of our careers. We may also be dealing with teenage children, aging parents, or both.

In our 50s, we may be thinking about retirement and preparing for the next stage of life. We may also be facing Empty Nest Syndrome as our children leave home.

In our 60s and beyond, we may be retired or semi-retired. We may also be facing health issues or caring for aging parents.

(For those of you *City Slicker*[14] fans out there, I hope you're not seeing this as another depressing Billy Crystal soliloquy here, although his take on the eras of life is one of the funniest I have ever seen.)

While none of the above dictate what will happen during different eras of your life — remember, there is no formula for predicting life — being sensitive to the impact of different eras helps as you consider your Priorities.

THE THREE LIFE STAGES

Closely associated with Eras is a concept I call the Three Life Stages. They are the Scout, the Warrior, and the Sage.

Scout – In the Scout stage, you are focused on learning and education, usually immersed in schooling, from the elementary level to higher education. You experience much of life for the very first time.

Like a Girl or Boy Scout, you're exploring and learning new things. You're in school, using dating apps, completing an internship, or participating in individual or team sports.

Friendships, personal growth/education, and hobbies/sports rank high as Priorities for you during this stage.

Warrior – In the Warrior stage, you focus on success and reputation. You've received diplomas and degrees and are now fully immersed in "adulting." The learning you gained as a Scout is now put to work, literally and figuratively.

You experience how tough life is (remember the bumper sticker?) and need to do battle during this stage — thus, the label Warrior. (And just for clarity, Warrior is not gender-specific, referring solely to men. Women are every bit the Warrior, even more so in many cases!)

As you become battle-tested, you often experience various kinds of success, including attaining prosperity in your finances, relationships, and community standing. You are likely engaged in a romantic relationship, raising/launching kids, building/succeeding in a career, and/or creating/maintaining wealth.

Work/career, money/wealth, children, and social standing tend to rank high in priority in this stage.

Sage – In the Sage stage, you are focused on influence and significance. By now, you have almost seen it all. At least, it feels that way. Your knowledge and reputation put you in a position where giving back becomes a strong focus.

You have fought battles and want to show others how it's done. You're not simply coasting into the sunset of your life. You are still peddling (though perhaps on an eBike), wanting to finish strong. You're often found volunteering with non-profits, grandparenting, engaged at church, and/or traveling.

Extended family, volunteering/altruism/community, health, and recreation tend to rank high in this stage, though all the higher-level commitments discussed earlier are attractive.

A Three-Dimensional View

The graphic on the right summarizes the Three Life Stages, though it requires you to view it three-dimensionally. For instance, think of the top of the graphic like a contact lens, convex in such a way that Influence is the center of the lens that slopes down through Reputation and Education. Below that is a three-dimensional cone that fans out from Sage to Warrior to Scout.

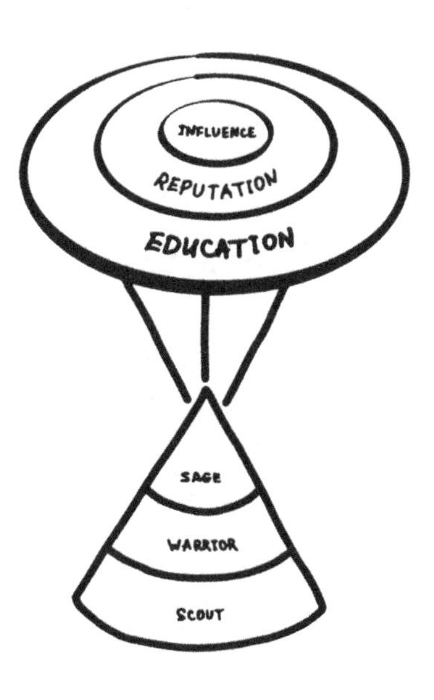

When you look down through the lens of Influence, the Sage stage is the focus; when looking down through the lens of Reputation, the Warrior stage is the focus; and when looking down through the lens of Education, the Scout stage is the focus. It is helpful to consider what stage of life you are in as you consider your Priorities.

My second-grade daughter was squarely in the Scout stage, where learning and education were primary. On that day in that parking lot, her top Priority was exploring peer-to-peer friendships.

On the other hand, I was in the Warrior stage, where fighting for my daughter's heart was my Priority. Knowing how impactful peer pressure can be and giving her space to grow was fighting for her heart. As was saying Hi to Dave, karaoke-ing to Rare Earth, and every so often, holding her hand.

It's essential to recognize that there are no bright lines about age regarding the Three Life Stages. The Stages are more aligned with wisdom and maturity than with age. The Stages can serve as an overlay for different periods in your life but are not intended to line up neatly with any specific age range.

The key is to consider what stage you may generally find yourself in and then determine what's important. How you do that is what we explore next.

TEASING OUT WHAT REALLY MATTERS

Imagine you're at the end of your life and have a chance to give your current self some advice on what's important and what matters. What would you say?

In his book *The Road to Character*, New York Times best-selling author David Brooks distinguishes between "résumé virtues" and "eulogy virtues"[15] as excellent guidance to help with this.

According to Brooks, résumé virtues are skills you bring to the marketplace. They make you a good fit for jobs and contribute to your success. You graduated college, are proficient with PowerPoint, and have supervised teams. These are résumé virtues.

Résumé virtues aren't bad in and of themselves, but when you step back from the hustle and bustle and rest on résumé virtues alone, you can often sense that something is missing. Something is amiss.

Résumé Virtues vs Eulogy Virtues

Eulogy virtues, on the other hand, foster purpose in a fragmented world. Eulogy virtues give life meaning, defining where you set your heart, mind, and Effort — your very existence.

Most of us avoid thinking about our eulogy virtues because we would have to think of death. But thinking about them can be empowering. Things that really matter come into focus.

It draws to mind the Tim McGraw song, *Live Like You Are Dying.* If you've ever listened to the lyrics, you'll know it tells the story of someone who learns they have a life-threatening illness. What did they do when they got the news? What follows is a list of things that suddenly mattered:

- Loving more deeply.
- Being a friend.
- Spending time with a dad.

It's a powerful song whose essence I bring to clients when I have them compose their own eulogies. Doing so creates a magnetic pull, drawing them to who they want to be. How to get there comes into focus, enabling them to break comfortable patterns, create new habits, and start moving toward a better future. (To go through a Eulogy Exercise on your own, go to https://rudiusstrategiesgroup.com/eulogy-exercise/.)

For instance, my client, Frank, wrote about his marriage and raising two kids in his eulogy. How he and his wife volunteered at their kids' schools and enjoyed all the swimming lessons and the soccer, basketball, and baseball games his kids played.

He also wrote about his extraordinary compassion to help others, investing earnings from his career in support of ministries, missionaries, and summer camps. In retirement, he taught financial literacy courses and did pro bono financial planning in underserved communities.

"With his quiet strength, courage, and kindness, he truly was a rock for the people around him," he wrote about himself.

Frank was single and just starting his career when we did this exercise together. It was easy for him to see the roadmap of what mattered in his life, both now and in the future. With it, we were able to work together and figure out what he needed to do now to make his words a reality in the future.

MAY FORCES BE WITH YOU

Coming up with our Priorities would be much easier if we lived in isolation. No outside influences to concern ourselves with, no one to answer to except ourselves.

But that's not reality.

Instead, not only are we made to be in relationship, we are, in fact, in relationships. And those relationships influence our Priorities as well.

Cultural Influences

For instance, we live in relationship with culture — the customs and social institutions of our country, people, social group, or family.

In a study that involved 500,000 surveys across 152 languages, researchers were able to compile data on what participants cared about in order to uncover what mattered most to people around the globe.[16] As could almost be expected, regardless of geography or culture, family ranked at or near the top of what mattered most.

But then the findings became more interesting.

Across all of Asia, for instance, social standing ranked high among participants, while not so much across the Americas, Africa, and the Middle East. Likewise, except for North America and Europe, the rest of the world ranked education as a high Priority. Undoubtedly much to the joy of everyone in the advertising industry in the so-called developed world, material possessions ranked high in North America and Europe. Meanwhile, that category ranked near the bottom in Africa and Oceania.

All of this points out the influence that culture has on our Priorities.

Relational Influences

In addition to cultural influences, relational influences also impact our Priorities. For instance, I'm married to an amazing woman. For over 30 years, we have done life together in a "two become one" kind of way. It's great, but it does complicate establishing Priorities.

Do I have my Priorities, and she has hers?

What happens when we have differing Priorities… and each feels strongly about their own?

Should we only have shared Priorities?

Wherever there are two parties in a relationship — be it husband-wife, parent-child, employer-employee, or government-citizen — it's crucial to be aware of the relational dynamics that each brings and incorporate them as best you can when setting your Priorities.

Intra-Relational Influences

We must also consider intra-relational influences. For instance, let's say that what matters most to you and your spouse is money/wealth. Intra-relational influences can be the different ways that we view money/wealth.

For example, you may have an abundance mindset, believing there's plenty out there for everybody. Others may have a scarcity mindset, thinking that what's out there is finite and limited. Neither is right; neither is wrong. But both will impact how we determine how important money/wealth is as a Priority.

We can explore similar intra-relational influences for all of our higher-level commitments, so it's valuable to be aware that intra-relational Priority complications exist.

SETTING OUR PRIORITIES

When it comes to "stuff," study after study has confirmed one common thing: We are hoarders. Acquiring and retaining stuff is our comfort food, and we don't like to discard anything.

In his book, *Subtract: The Untapped Science of Less*, Leidy Klotz points out, "We collect new-and-improved ideas, but don't prune the outdated ones. Every day, across challenges big and small, we neglect a basic way to make things better: We don't subtract."[17]

In other words, we pile into to-do's but don't consider stop-doings.

Klotz's idea is less is more — the concept of addition by subtraction. So rather than continuously adding more and more to your life, it would be best if you considered doing with less. Instead of pursuing all fifteen of the higher-level commitments, narrow it down to the two or three most appropriate for where you are.

A way to go about this is through simplicity and presence.

Simplicity – All too often, you get stuck being busy but not accomplishing anything. You set your intentions, then reset your intentions, then reset them again, never to see the outcome. You make resolutions, then break them, only to then try again.

The more you simplify your life, the easier it is to set Priorities.

For example, when you have fewer things on your plate, you can focus on what matters. You eliminate frustration when you declutter and simplify, including narrowing your higher-level Priorities to two or three key ones applicable to your life stage and life events.

Presence – It's easy to get caught up in the past or future and lose sight of what's happening right now. You are so involved in activity that you are not present. But if you want to set Priorities that reflect what matters, you need to be present in the moment.

Being present means creating space and time for yourself — not just physical space, but mental space. You can't set Priorities if you don't know what you want or need. That's why it's essential to make time for yourself. Once you create space and become present, you can start asking questions about what's most important, which I highlighted earlier in this chapter.

It's not easy to set Priorities on your own. We often get stuck in the have-to of the right now. So, we fail to uncover what it is that really matters.

You can't set Priorities if you don't know what you want or need. That's why it's essential to make time for yourself.

Often, it helps to talk to someone who can offer impartial advice and help you figure out what's most important.

That can be a friend, a family member, or even a professional coach (shameless plug). Whoever it ends up being with, please do it.

Finally, it's important to give yourself grace to take the time needed to explore. Priorities are important, but finding, setting, and balancing them isn't an exact science. There is no straightforward process to follow. You are imperfect and will make mistakes. That's OK. Have faith in the process and trust that things will work out over time. There is no formula. Making adjustments is part of life and definitely part of the Delta Theorem.

We don't live with purpose, on purpose based solely on Priorities. We also must know what we stand for, which is where we are going next. But first, let's end this chapter with an exercise to help define your Priorities.

SHOW UP | ENGAGE | DO THE WORK

Take some time to answer the following:

1. What is most important to me in my life?

2. What values drive my actions and decisions?

3. What do I want to accomplish or achieve in the short term and long term?

4. What activities or tasks bring me the most joy, satisfaction, or fulfillment?

5. What are the things that I need to do on a daily or weekly basis to maintain my health, well-being, and quality of life?

6. What are the things that I am most motivated to pursue?

7. What are the things that I feel most obligated to do or responsible for doing?

CHAPTER 3

Principles as Our Points of Leverage

"Our principles are the springs of our actions; our actions, the springs of our happiness or misery. Too much care, therefore, cannot be taken in forming our principles."
— Philip Skelton

IN EARLY 2012, I found myself at something of a career crossroads. I had just experienced what I thought would never happen: I was fired. And it wasn't fun.

After a few months of recovering from that stinger, I saw a LinkedIn posting that grabbed me. A family office in the Northeast was looking for a head of operations, a role I thought I could crush. I quickly sent my résumé, hoping for the best.

Not long after, I got a call from an executive recruiter asking if I knew anything about the firm doing the search, Bridgewater

Associates, or its founder, Ray Dalio. I knew Bridgewater as a hedge fund that made investors boatloads of money, and I had heard that Dalio created a **very** unique culture there, but not more than that.

After hanging up, I did some research.

I then learned of Bridgewater's "principle-based approach" to pretty much everything. They had a culture of radical transparency where open and honest dialogue — brutally honest most times — was not only encouraged but demanded. I also got my hands on a set of the principles that Dalio himself wrote as the playbook for how Bridgewater operated, the same principles he later published in his 2017 bestselling book, *Principles*.[18]

I was blown away.

Never had I seen anything like what I read. The detail Dalio laid out was astounding. Practicality on every page. And there were lots of pages. Things like "Pain + Reflection = Progress" and "Own your outcomes."

It was clear to me the tremendous value Dalio created by putting his principles to paper.

As it turned out, Bridgewater didn't think I could crush the role as much as I did. After several rounds of dialogue, I didn't land the position. However, I did land something even more impactful on my future: The power of well-documented principles toward simplifying and improving decision-making. Dalio and Bridgewater were unambiguous proof.

LEVERAGE: WHAT ARE WE EVEN TALKING ABOUT?

Archimedes of Syracuse was a philosopher and mathematician from the 2nd century BC who some consider the greatest mathematician of ancient history. As one of the first to apply theories from math to explain the movement of physical objects, he is well-known for having said, "Give me a place to stand, and I will move the whole earth with a lever." It was his precursor to the Theory of the Lever, where he proposed that when a rigid beam is balanced on a fulcrum, it could lift proportionally much greater weight than the force applied.

The power, or the leverage, was in the fixed positioning of the fulcrum with reference to the beam. With proper positioning of the fulcrum and the right length of the beam, any object could be lifted by another object a fraction of the size. And it works.

It's a good analogy when considering Principles in the Delta Theorem.

In a broad sense, Principles are the fixed fulcrum points of decision-making. They are the overarching standards you live by, and thus, they direct your choices. Without Principles, you may be prone to confusion and indecision.

Like fulcrums, Principles serve as the leverage points upon which choices are made. You check yourself against them to determine if an action is acceptable or right. They can be helpful when you have difficult decisions to make, particularly when your emotions are involved.

When you're thinking through options for your choices, Principles allow you to project the long-range consequences of different courses of action. You then turn to them as reliable shortcuts for problem-solving and decision-making.

KEY CHARACTERISTICS OF PRINCIPLES

For Ray Dalio, Principles integrate and explain reality. As he described in *Principles*, "All the laws of reality were given to us by nature. Man didn't create these laws, but by understanding them, we can use them to foster our own evolution and achieve our goals."[19] The key is finding ones that perfectly address that reality. Those that do have two key characteristics: First, they're universal, and second, they explain cause and effect.

By "universal," I mean they are fundamental truths that apply to all conditions and circumstances. Logically, this has to be true. You wouldn't have a principle that works in one situation but not another. That's just stupid, and we know what being stupid does to make life harder than it already is.

But Principles are also reasonable explanations for the cause-and-effect relationship in your choices. The very term "cause" implies an answer to a "why" question. Why did this happen? Why did that happen? The "this" and the "that" are effects, and the answer is the cause.

For instance, gravity is a well-established principle with universal characteristics and explains cause and effect. When you throw a ball in the air, it will return to earth. It always happens (universal), and there's a cause (earth's pull) and effect (ball comes down). Voilà, the principle of gravity.

With your life Principles, you are looking for similar universal and causal standards that fully address your realities.

RULES VS. STANDARDS

A lot of us think of principles as rules. I don't. Rules are constraining and rigid. They're authoritative, usually dictated from above in a top-down way. They often come from rulers, and none of us likes to be subjects of rulers. And perhaps even more importantly, rule-following sucks the life right out of most people.

No one enjoys being told, "Well, like it or not, this is how things go here. These are the rules we follow." So, while it might be good to know the rules for board games when you're playing them, it's not helpful for feeling alive.

Standards, on the other hand, are less constraining. With standards, you have a greater range of choice. While still authoritative, standards provide more flexibility for balancing several factors. They're not so rigid but are more open-ended, providing a way to make decisions that are right for you. They help you assess different situations and determine the best course of action.

You participate in the development of standards. They're not dictated to you like you must check your mind at the door and follow them blindly. By developing them, you also develop more of a sense of ownership and empowerment.

None of this is to imply that just because rules come from others, they ought never to be adopted as life principles. Often, principles that have been handed down to us from culture or upbringing can serve as powerful standards for our life. The 10 Commandments from the Bible are a great example. They address realities in a universal and causal manner.

This is also true for many spiritual and other texts available to us. The *Quran*, the *Bhagavad Gita*, and even the U.S. Constitution are but some of the many real-life examples of these.

I tend to gravitate toward standards that are simple and practical. For instance, here's one set that is simple, practical, and powerful.

LEGENDARY PRINCIPLES

Sometime in the 1920s, a rural Indiana farmer handed his son a piece of paper with seven handwritten principles, a piece of paper that the boy was known to keep in his wallet until the day he died. Those principles were:

- Be true to yourself.
- Help others.
- Make each day your masterpiece.
- Drink deeply from good books, especially the Bible.
- Make friendship a fine art.
- Build a shelter against a rainy day by the life you live.
- Pray for guidance and counsel, and give thanks for your blessings each day.[20]

The farmer's name was Joshua Wooden. And his son was the legendary college basketball coach, John Wooden.

John Wooden coached his UCLA men's basketball teams to ten national championships over a twelve-year period. That included an inconceivable seven titles in a row… seven in a row!… as well as a record 88 consecutive wins. During his tenure, no one even came close to beating the Bruins.

But for those who knew him, success on the basketball court was not what made Wooden so legendary. It was his character as a man.

"I have always tried to make it clear that basketball is not the ultimate," he would say. "It is of small importance in comparison to the total life we live." His life proved this to be the case.

In 1948, well before his success on the basketball court, Wooden created the "Pyramid of Success," a list of 25 common principles that laid out a path to becoming a better person, a path directly influenced by that note from his father.

Giants Because of Principles

I hope by now it's evident how important Principles were in the successes of Ray Dalio and John Wooden. The truth is, these men are but two of the many examples we could shine a light on.

But don't dare fall into the trap of dismissing the impact Principles can have on your life just because Dalio and Wooden are "giants" while we are mere mortals. That would be to miss the point entirely.

The Dalios and Woodens of the world don't use Principles because they're giants. They're giants because they use Principles. I believe we can be, too.

> The Dalios and Woodens of the world don't use Principles because they're giants. They're giants because they use Principles.

With every good thing, though, there always seems to be a shadow. Principles are no exception. Those shadows are where we turn next.

SHADOW SIDES OF PRINCIPLES

Given how valuable Principles are for life, it's worth looking at their shadow sides. Each of these undermines the power of Principles and causes you to question their purpose and effectiveness.

Ethical Dilemmas: Many people follow common standards as Principles. We already mentioned the Ten Commandments as a set. Some other common ones include:

- Every individual has certain inalienable rights that must be respected. (Principle of Rights)
- People should be treated equitably and fairly. (Principle of Justice)
- What is good for the individual must also be good for society. (Principle of the Common Good)
- The correct action is the one that maximizes the greatest amount of good for the greatest number of people. (Principle of Utility)
- Certain actions are intrinsically right or wrong. (Principle of Duty)

It's probable that you hold firmly to all five. Most of us do. While these are excellent standards to follow, they can sometimes leave you in something of a quandary, given the potential for conflict between them.

For example, it is widely accepted that murder is intrinsically wrong (Principle of Duty); however, there's the death penalty (Principle of Justice), which many argue is murder.

Conflict. Dilemma.

Or take the case where you knowingly hire undocumented workers. Certainly, breaking the law by hiring someone who is an illegal alien is intrinsically wrong (Principle of Duty), but doesn't the worker have an inalienable right to life, liberty, and the pursuit of happiness (Principle of Rights)?

It is easy to see how ethical dilemmas arising from seemingly conflicting universal standards can cause questions about living by Principles.

Relativism: I defined Principles as universal rules that operate under all conditions and in all circumstances. In other words, they are standards that are always true and fixed regardless of time, place, and the people concerned — the very definition of an absolute.

But when it comes to actual situations, there's a school of thought that says standards are not permanently fixed but depend on the context of the circumstances. Things are relative. There are too many gray areas involving cultural and diversity differences for something to be absolute. So, it's easy to see how this can undermine a commitment to living by Principles.

I ran into a somewhat hilarious form of this in earning my coaching certification.

Cheaters Never Prosper?

To be certified, my coaching program required completing a Navy SEAL-style crucible event involving 12 straight hours of pushing my limits physically, mentally, and emotionally. From 6 a.m. to 6 p.m. one Monday in March, my fellow coaching cohort and I were challenged to see how we applied the tools we were trained in within our program.

We were pounded in Pacific Ocean surf, hammered hiking up a mountain with sandbag-filled backpacks, and blasted completing a MURPH—1-mile run, 100 pull-ups, 200 pushups, 300 air squats, and another 1-mile run, all within a 75-minute time limit. And that's to say nothing about the burpees (cross-fit exercises involving dynamic pushups), the sugar cookies (get wet and roll in the sand so it covers every possible centimeter of your body), and the flutter kicks we did throughout the 12-hour grind.

It was glorious... **not**.

About halfway into the event, one of the leaders offered a "principle" to consider, giving us a little chuckle at the time: "It ain't cheatin' if you don't get caught."

By then, each of us was dog-tired and knew we had a long way to go. We all started giving it some genuine thought. "Was he serious?

Was this something others used before to get through these things? Was it legit to use?"

It was easy to see the slight advantage we might gain if we fudged even just a little. And every advantage mattered. Trust me. But if we got caught… well, just don't get caught!

I won't tell you whether we did or didn't cheat. (Or whether I did or didn't.) That's not the point. The point is to consider Principles and relativism.

Is cheating always wrong regardless of time, place, and the people concerned? We tell our kids so. But what if the circumstances warrant it? Even encourage it?

And does relativism render living with Principles wrong? Or even stupid? Those are the undermining questions relativism creates.

One final thing on relativism.

When taken to its end, relativism tends to land as political correctness — speaking so as not to offend or marginalize anyone — what used to be called "good manners." When looked at from that perspective, political correctness isn't a bad thing. But that assumes we're speaking to each other at all. And when we speak, we do so freely, especially about what we feel is right. Or even wrong. Our Principles.

Unfortunately, today's political correctness is causing us to speak less and less to each other, dangerously close to the place where the only universal principle is to have no Principles at all.

Tyrants: It's easy to point to tyrants who have used Principles to justify bad behavior or to manipulate and control. Pick a tyrant, any tyrant. Research their justifications for their actions. We don't have to name names. Some acted out of deliberate self-interest, advantaging themselves while putting others at a distinct disadvantage.

But most tyrants tend to honestly believe they are acting out of principle. And they may very well be, though likely, either from wrong Principles (there are such things) or misguided application.

There are also those tyrants who follow Principles with such strict adherence that they're impossible to be around. They follow a strict "letter of the law" over a more gracious "spirit of the law." These tyrants tend to suck us dry.

One such "letter of the law" tyrant is the fanatic police inspector, Javert, from Victor Hugo's masterpiece, *Les Misérables.*[21]

In Hugo's story, Jean Valjean is a man who did nineteen years of hard labor for stealing a loaf of bread. Finally paroled, he pursues an honest life, but not before taking on a new identity to avoid going back to prison after a minor infraction. He is a truly good and principled man who uttered these unforgettable words at the end of his life, "It is nothing to die; it is dreadful not to live."

Valjean lives from a freed heart.

On the other hand, Javert is a man possessed by devotion to the law, completely rigid and inflexible. An unyielding pursuit of justice causes him to dog Jean Valjean throughout all of Valjean's days.

Javert lives as a broken man. Though he eventually has a brief moment of redemption at the story's end, he is nonetheless the epitome of the heartless tyrant, so caught up in law, morality, and rigid principle that he becomes a slave to them.

It's not my purpose to debate the pros and cons of each of the above shadows of Principles. Certainly, you must be careful not to use Principles as a weapon or justification for bad behavior. And when it comes to decision-making, Principles are not the be-all, end-all. But they do play a key role in living life with purpose, on purpose, as vitally important guides to help you make the best choices in life. It's up to you to find your own correct balance in living them out.

DISCOVERING OUR PRINCIPLES

Suppose we are in a coaching session together, and I ask you the following questions: What is the foundational set of standards that are the non-negotiables in your life? What do you stand for?

Would you be able to answer those right then and there? Unfortunately, most of us can't.

Most of us have never taken the time to consider the Principles that guide our actions, let alone rattle them off. We certainly have not taken the time to write them down. But given what an essential role they play in life, it's vital to have and know our Principles and be conscious of them at all times.

An excellent place to start is through an introspective process I take my clients through.

1. Identify the behaviors you want in the ideal version of yourself.

Visualize the person you see yourself as. Not a perfect person, but the person you see as characteristic of how you show up in the world.

Now think of some of the actual situations you face and the choices that will likely need to be made. Roles you currently play. Spouse. Parent. Employee. Business Owner. Student. In any particular role, what is a likely scenario you will face?

The best Principles are the ones that cover multiple roles and situations.

For instance, in the role of spouse, you are likely to face a situation where your faithfulness to the relationship could be tested. Think of a universal cause-and-effect action that would apply to the situation. "If I am unfaithful to my spouse, my life will be chaotic." You then may adopt the principle, "Thou shalt not commit adultery," converting something you may have thought was forced upon you based on your upbringing (one of the Ten Commandments from the Bible) to a foundational truth to live by. This can be done for any roles you play and situations you may face.

A word of caution, however.

Certainly, we can't do this for every situation or role we find ourselves in. A good thing to do is search for opportunities to bundle roles and situations to find common threads. Then identify Principles that cover multiple situations and roles.

For instance, you will be asked to take on a responsibility across several roles and situations. You can consider that "once I give my response, my reputation will be at stake. I want a good reputation, no matter whom I relate to." Universal cause and effect.

You could then determine that a principle to live by would be "Let my Yes be yes, and my No be no." In doing so, you make your word your bond (Yes be yes), yet still have the flexibility not to do everything (No be no).

2. Identify values that are important to you.

Values describe what is indispensable in your life, unconsciously helping you form your individual Principles. They are central to human flourishing. You need to define and understand your values if you want to live with personal integrity.

If you are not sure of your values, you are not alone. We often don't take the time to consider our personal values because we are busy conforming to the values of others. However, since Principles follow from personal values, identifying a list of your top values is a great starting place.

One of the easiest ways to assess your values is through a simple evaluation. Just ask how important a set of different values are, then evaluate across a scale from Not Important to Very Important, numbering the scale from 1 to 5 as follows:

Not Important	Slightly Important	Important	Fairly Important	Very Important
1	2	3	4	5

Once you are done with the evaluation, go through your answers and list your top 5 highest scoring values, then rank those in order of importance. So, your most important value would be number 1, your second most important value would be number 2, etc. Then you'll have your top values. From there, you can start thinking of Principles that align with those values.

Here is a good list of common values to start with:

Common Values

- Loyalty
- Kindness
- Courage
- Compassion
- Honesty
- Spirituality
- Integrity
- Tolerance
- Determination
- Generosity
- Humility
- Selflessness
- Trustworthy
- Equanimity
- Altruism

Many years ago, I went through this process for myself. After a period of trial and error, I was able to narrow down my Principles directly from my values as follows:

- Fear the Lord as the beginning of knowledge. (Faith)
- Do unto others as you would have them do unto you. (Reciprocity)
- Ensure character counts every moment, every day. (Integrity)
- Take extreme ownership. (Accountability)

- Be the subject, not the object. (Proactivity)
- Champion the power of we. (Teamwork)
- Seek the uncommon. (Risk)
- No retreat; the obstacle is the way. (Perseverance)
- Be an infinite learner. (Curiosity)
- Get away from it all. (Rest)

3. Get inspired by other sources.

Think of the things you believe in and for which you will take a stand. What comes to mind? Interestingly enough, we often find it easier to define ourselves by what we are against rather than what we are for.

Now think of some sources of inspiration that have influenced your thinking over the years. Parents. Teachers. Religious texts. Books. Even movies and music.

What are some of the more memorable inspirations that come to mind?

Here are but a few examples that may prime your thinking:

Examples of Sources for Principles

Source	Principles
Spiritual Texts	Thou shalt not steal. — *Holy Bible* Do not mix the truth with falsehood or conceal the truth while you know it. — *Quran*
Quotes	Whether you think you can or think you can't, you're right. — *Henry Ford* Success is walking from failure to failure with no loss of enthusiasm. — *Winston Churchill*

Movies	What we do in life echoes in eternity. — *Gladiator* Do or do not. There is no try. — *The Empire Strikes Back*
Books/ Literature	The one thing that doesn't abide by majority rule is a person's conscience. — *To Kill a Mockingbird* Anything worth dying for is certainly worth living for. — *Catch-22*
Poetry	Two roads diverged in a wood, and I — I took the one less traveled by. — *The Road Not Taken* We loved with a love that was more than love. — *Annabel Lee*

When you identify the meaningful or memorable inspirations that come to you, you regularly find that these are the fundamental Principles you live by.

Most importantly, the inspirations must be yours, not someone else's. Sure, you may have been taught them or learned them from others, but they are only your true Principles when they represent the things you will stay true to in your life.

By now, I trust you see how important having and knowing your Principles are to your life. Before we look at Passion, work through these questions to clarify your Principles.

SHOW UP | ENGAGE | DO THE WORK

Take some time to answer the following:

1. What values or beliefs are most important to me?

2. What do I stand for or believe in strongly?

3. What are the things I will not compromise on or deviate from, no matter what?

4. What are the things that I believe are most important for a fulfilling and meaningful life?

5. What are the things that I believe are most important for a just and fair society?

6. What are the things that I believe are most important for the well-being and happiness of myself and others?

7. What do I believe is right or wrong, and why?

CHAPTER 4

Passion as a Flame

"Finding your passion isn't just about careers and money. It's about finding your authentic self, the one you've buried beneath other people's needs."

— Anonymous

GO TO ANY commencement ceremony these days, and there's at least a 50% chance you will hear the keynote speaker use one of these simple yet bold phrases:

- Be passionate.
- Have passion for what you do.
- Follow your passion.

Each, in their own way, places great confidence in this one seemingly overused concept: Passion.

And it's not just at graduations where these phrases are being used. Whether it be parenting, career counseling, or even coaching, everywhere you turn, the road of passion seems the most emphasized road to happiness, contentment, and growth.

Having just "launched" a twenty-something daughter, I can tell you firsthand those phrases have influenced my own parenting. As a dad, it's hard not to default to that great-sounding advice, "Do what you love, and you'll never work a day in your life." In other words, have passion for what you do, follow it, and you'll love your life. (And you'll be off my payroll.)

Unfortunately, it's not the best advice; in fact, it's almost dangerous.

First, these mantras assume you have preexisting passion — as if it exists from birth and would practically ooze out of you if you tip over. And second, they assume that if you match passion to what you do, you're almost guaranteed to have a carefree and successful life.

Unfortunately, neither of these is true.

At the same time, there's something about the advice that's not all bad either. Many great thinkers throughout history, people like Hagel and Descartes, have seen the tremendous value passion has to offer.

THE VALUE OF PASSION

Often, passion is the energy that keeps you going, an energy that keeps you filled with meaning, happiness, excitement, and anticipation. It can be a driving force behind success and happiness, helping you live a better life.

For example, a 2015 study published in *The Annals of Behavioral Medicine* found that pursuing passion lowers stress and contributes to greater overall happiness[22].

Given how subjective a concept it is, you must understand what Passion is, its benefits, its common categorizations, its different types, and how it can be discovered.

WHAT IS PASSION?

There are many descriptions of passion floating around these days. Some describe it as the flame that burns inside, compelling you to do the things you love. And not just the things you fall in love with — but the stuff you stay in love with.

Take former professional football player Al "Bubba" Baker.

Bubba Baker grew up in a large family where barbecue-style cooking was practically the only thing on the menu, and if you didn't learn to cook, you didn't eat. So, he quickly learned how to cook the best barbecue around.

When his football playing days ended, Baker started a food company that included his restaurant, Bubba's-Q World-famous Bar-B-Que & Catering, and a patented way for people to eat fully cooked, deboned barbeque ribs with a knife and fork. In 2013, he pitched his company on the TV show *Shark Tank,* where venture capitalist Daymond John agreed to become a partner.

Others see passion as a love for activities that bring joy to our lives. Often, they're hobbies or sports with which you have some strong attraction or emotional connection.

Consider Yvon Chouinard, founder of the outdoor clothing and gear company Patagonia. Chouinard was an avid mountaineer who had a passion for the outdoors. To save money, he began making his own climbing tools, teaching himself blacksmithing in the process. But that was not all. Chouinard also had the wish to design clothing that was suitable for rock and alpine climbing. From there, Patagonia was born.

These days, the brand is known globally as an environmentally conscious gear and apparel company that encourages its employees to "get out there and do something great for the planet."

Still, others consider passion the drive that keeps moving a person forward in all they are and do. Different from motivation, drive gets us to what we want. It keeps us going when motivation ebbs and flows.

In 1989, while an undergrad at Princeton, for instance, Wendy Kopp wrote a senior thesis proposing a Teachers Corps similar in concept to the Peace Corps from the 60s. Her time at Princeton made her aware that students from disadvantaged communities came to college less prepared than those from more affluent areas. She believed sending highly qualified teachers into these communities was the answer.

Needing funding but convinced that her peers would be willing to choose volunteer teaching opportunities over more lucrative opportunities to make a difference in the world, she doggedly pursued anyone interested in improving education, sending her thesis to scores of corporate executives and philanthropists. But it was her persistent effort in recruiting teacher volunteers that captured attention, leading to the founding of Teach For America, a network that now boasts 58,000 alums in over 50 regions in the U.S. alone.

"I had this idea that this was going to change the consciousness of the country," Kopp said.[23] And in many ways, it has.

PASSION AS FOCUSED DESIRE

When I think of Passion in relation to the Delta Theorem, I think of it as focused desire: a preoccupation with something we love, something that makes us feel most alive. It's consistent over time. It involves risk. You live and breathe it with greater intensity than mere enthusiasm.

That's because Passion is more than intense emotion. It's ingrained in your body and soul.

> Passion is more than intense emotion. It's ingrained in your body and soul.

In the words of author John Eldredge in his book *Journey of Desire*, "Desire (passion) can lead us to the life we were meant to live. And desire can get us into a heap of trouble, too."[24]

One of the best examples of this focused desire comes from the life of legendary women's tennis champion Billie Jean King.

FOCUS OF A CHAMPION

One of the most prestigious events in all of sport is the Wimbledon Championships, the oldest tennis tournament in the world. Since 1877, spectators from all over the world have gathered in Wimbledon, England, annually to watch the best tennis players battle for coveted titles in singles, doubles, and mixed doubles.

One of the greatest players of all time is Billie Jean King.

During her heyday, Billie Jean King won a record 20 career titles at Wimbledon — six in singles, 10 in women's doubles, and four in mixed doubles. Late in her career, though, King had to come to grips with the inevitable: her mastery of the game was declining, and younger players were catching up with her.

In her memoir, King reflected on one of her last times playing Wimbledon, providing us with a glimpse of focused desire in action:

> Of course, I can just say I want to win all three—the singles, doubles, and mixed. Easy to say and easy to want, but so difficult to execute. How can I do it? More than

> anything else, I must love everything that is part and parcel of the total Wimbledon scene. I must love hitting that little white ball; love every strain of running and bending those tired knees; love every bead of sweat; love every cloud or every ray of sun in the sky; love every moment of tension, waiting in the locker room; love the lack of total rest every night, the hunger pains during the day, practicing on the outside court with your stomach in your throat before the match; love watching people queue, knowing some of them are feeling the tension in the air; love feeling and absorbing the tradition of almost one hundred years. In essence, I have to possess enough passion and love to withstand all the odds. No matter how tough, no matter what kind of outside pressure, no matter how many bad breaks along the way, I must keep my sights on the final goal, to win, win, win —and with more love and passion than the world has ever witnessed in any performance.[25]

For King, it wasn't just a love of all things Wimbledon. It was a Passion for being on top. For winning. That was her focus.

And winning didn't just come to her because she had a driving desire for it. King had to risk. And she had to show up, engage, and do the work.

In a day and age where attention spans are getting shorter and shorter, the focus that Passion creates may be the greatest benefit it offers. But there are many more.

THE BENEFITS OF PASSION

The benefits that Passion offers are many. For instance, Passion generates and inspires hard work, curiosity, and confidence. The more passionate you are, the more fervent you are, creating an optimistic outlook. Billie Jean King certainly had it. As did Walt Disney.

As successful as Walt Disney ultimately became, it is little known that he launched several failed animation companies. Knowing that he had what it took to be a successful animator, his focused desire inspired him to stay confident and press on, ultimately leading to the creation of Mickey Mouse in 1928.

Passion also boosts your discipline. As you pursue Passion in a career, for instance, you put in the hard work necessary to be successful while contributing to the workplace.

Similarly, as you pursue interests outside of work, you develop and maintain a healthy work-life balance, reaping many advantages: enhanced mental health, more engagement, and a happier and less stressed life.

When you have little to no Passion for what you do for a living, it's tough to push through hard times. Passion supports persevering through challenges. With it, you are more apt to overlook hardship and strive to improve.

For instance, having a strong work ethic and knowing that your work pays the bills helps, but having Passion for what you do provides a deeper incentive and motive to stick with things and see them through.

Passion also helps you make decisions based on what matters most to you. Take something as trivial as how you choose to be entertained.

With the proliferation of content and viewing options, it can be practically overwhelming to scan through the thousands of movies and TV shows to determine what to watch. Passion can serve as a "highlighter" for your brain, focusing your attention on content that matters.

Now that we have explored what Passion is and taken a look at its benefits, it makes sense to take an even deeper dive into it. And there's no better place to start than looking at some of the most common distinctions for where to find your Passion.

COMMON PASSIONS

Most of us would love to follow our Passion if we only knew what it actually looked like. But, having not yet cracked the Passion "code," we feel pressured to find our Passion, fearing that by not doing so, we may live lives of, as Henry David Thoreau put it, "quiet desperation."

We place so much pressure on ourselves that we may pursue every idea out there. Or we get so overwhelmed and think that what we're currently doing will have to be enough.

I'm no different. When I set out to explore Passion, I felt that same pressure. But the more I dug in, the more I recognized that Passion usually fits into one of the following broad areas of focus:

- ***Fitness*** – A Passion for fitness includes all physical wellness — not just how we work out or how we eat, but also how we sleep and recover.
- ***Relationship*** – Motivational speaker Jim Rohn famously said that we are the average of the five people we spend the most time with. A Passion for relationship involves the strong desire to create reciprocal appreciation and respect in our personal connections.
- ***Self-improvement*** – Those passionate about self-improvement have an in-depth interest in helping themselves in order to help others. My Passion for self-improvement led to the development of the Delta Theorem and this book's writing.
- ***Creativity*** – Artists, actors, painters, sculptors, musicians, directors, writers — the list is expansive — all share a focused desire to create new things. They love to buck trends, come up with new ideas or ways of doing things, and share that creativity with a broader audience.
- ***Entrepreneurship*** – Closely associated with creativity, a Passion for entrepreneurship is a focused desire to forge our

own paths in business. This focused desire is typically not about money but rather about the freedom of doing something we enjoy and find challenging that demands risk.

- ***Learning*** – The intense enjoyment of experiencing new thoughts and teaching others isn't limited to academia; it's also found in leadership positions where the desire to guide others is of the utmost importance.
- ***Transcendence*** – For many, spiritual practices like prayer or contemplation, or being involved with communities of faith, provides deep emotional connection and joy to life. So much impact on the world, both good and not-so-good, comes from a Passion for transcendence.
- ***Humanitarianism*** –Some of the most noteworthy people of all time… the Mother Teresas, the Jane Goodalls, the Martin Luther King, Jrs.… all had this Passion for making the world better. It often involves recognizing injustices, working for the environment, or promoting positive social change.
- ***Simplification*** – Simplification usually focuses on recreational activities that reduce stress, allowing us to focus on Priorities more efficiently. Prioritizing activities we find calming, like sailing or meditation, or even downsizing and more minimalist living, can ensure the right headspace to tackle the curveballs that life is constantly throwing at us.

Many other strong interests also qualify as Passions. For instance, you might have such an intense love for animals that you consider it your Passion. Similarly, you may be devoted to a particular sport or sports team that you think of as your Passion. While you can be passionate about these things, they tend to be encompassed within one or more of the broader categories above, so I don't separate them for application purposes in the Delta Theorem.

You may have also noted that I did not include career as a common area. Many people consider career as their ultimate Passion. While that can be true, I don't include it because it's practically implied since we often make careers out of the common Passions listed above.

That being said, below is a general listing of some roles closely associated with the categories, many of which we make careers out of:

Category	Roles
Fitness	Athlete, Trainer, Nutritionist
Relationship	Spouse/Partner, Parent, Friend, Colleague
Self-improvement	Counselor, Writer, Mentor, Speaker
Creativity	Artist, Musician, Actor, Director
Entrepreneurship	Founder, Executive, Innovator, Disruptor
Learning	Teacher, Student, Leader
Transcendence	Pastor, Rabbi, Yogi, Believer
Humanitarianism	Philanthropist, Welfare Worker, Environmentalist
Simplification	Minimalist, Guide, Hobbyist

THE TWO TYPES OF PASSION

In the early 2000s, a Canadian research team conducted four studies involving over 900 participants looking at the concept of passion. In their findings, they identified two different types of passion: harmonious passion and obsessive passion.[26] Both are worth taking a look at.

Harmonious Passion

The researchers described harmonious passion as the type of passion that is in balance with other areas of living. It is proportional to all life. It provides for exploration and engagement in activity for the pleasure of the process, remaining flexible and open-minded along the way.

With harmonious passion, you choose to engage in activity freely, contributing to positive outcomes. Similarly, if you were to decide not to engage in an activity that was the object of your harmonious passion, it wouldn't impact your sense of self or well-being in any negative way.

Positive psychological function, physical health, and satisfaction were all linked to harmonious passion.

One reason for these positive links is that with harmonious passion, you can often act in a state of flow, having a sense of harmony or fluidity between your mind and body. Many call it being "in the zone," a state we've all likely experienced at some point in life.

It is a state where you filter out background noise, do not notice the passage of time, and get lost in what you do. Reality shifts slightly, with a heightened sense of awareness or concentration, and you feel totally in control.

Distance runners experience it, for instance, during long runs, as do computer programmers while enmeshed in coding projects. (We'll talk more about flow when we talk about Effort in Chapter 6.)

On the other hand, the research unearthed another kind of passion: obsessive passion.

Obsessive Passion

Obsessive passion is the type of passion that becomes all-consuming, compulsive, and even dominating. It's the shadow side of harmonious passion.

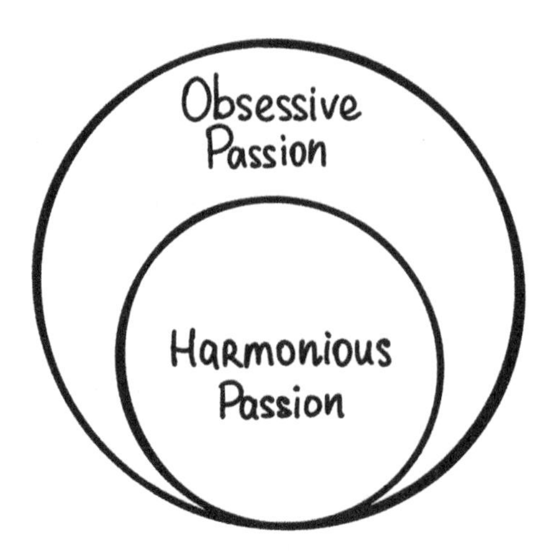

A passion becomes obsessive and problematic when you relentlessly pursue an activity with such rigid persistence that you lose all sense of self-control. The object of obsessive passion becomes the primary focus of life, negatively impacting your other activities or relationships. It's no longer a passion, but a compulsion, and burnout is often the result.

To illustrate their findings, the research team used the example of a university professor with a passion for playing the guitar (a focused desire towards creativity) who was invited to join friends and create music together the night before giving an important lecture.

With harmonious passion for his guitar playing, the professor can easily tell his friends that he'll take a rain check, so he can fully engage in preparing the talk. He is still passionate about creating music but feels no fear of missing out (FOMO) on the jam session.

Likewise, if the professor could attend the session with no obligation the following day, he would do so, very likely enjoying the time so much to enter the state of guitar playing flow.

In addition, with harmonious passion, if he decided it had become a permanent negative factor in his life, he would have the control to stop playing guitar altogether. His passion for guitar playing would be harmonizing with the rest of his life.

On the other hand, the guitar-loving professor with obsessive passion might not be able to resist an invitation to jam with friends. He could not help but engage in the activity. Thus, when confronted with the possibility of jamming with his friends or preparing for the next day's lecture, the professor would find himself without self-control, unable to say no.

During the jam session, though, he might feel upset for playing music instead of preparing the talk, perhaps having difficulties focusing on the task at hand (playing the music). He likely would experience less positive affect than he would like.

Even worse, because he neglected to adequately prepare for the lecture, his performance on that would likely suffer, or he could fail miserably, thus creating all kinds of havoc in his life. Either way, the obsessive passion led to negative consequences.

Remember, life is tough; it's even tougher if you're stupid. Obsessive Passion is stupid.

What we're after when using the Delta Theorem is harmonious Passion, the kind that's harmonizing with the other elements of the Theorem, namely Principles and Priorities. The type of Passion that is filled with wisdom.

Hopefully, by now, I've convinced you to see the value and importance of Passion. But not just any Passion. Passion that reflects our focused desires. Yet, what do we do if we find ourselves with no real Passion at all?

While there's a chance Passion might exist but be buried by layers of responsibilities, relationships, or others' expectations of us, we know we can't just go looking for Passion and suddenly have it appear. It's more likely that it needs to be grown and cultivated. It's a process of discovery. And the place to start is to look at what brings us intrinsic enjoyment: our interests.

DISCOVERING PASSION

Research has indicated that we're much more satisfied when doing things that fit our interests. Pursuing interests makes us feel good and contributes to our overall happiness. And, when cultivated, those interests ultimately become our Passion.

But the process of interest discovery is usually slow, messy, and filled with the unexpected. We can't predict with certainty what will or won't capture our attention. And simply willing ourselves to be interested in things doesn't work either. Instead, finding our Passion is a process of trial and error, discovery, and cultivation.

> Finding our Passion is a process of trial and error, discovery, and cultivation.

In her book *Grit*, Angela Duckworth captures the essence of what it means to discover our interests and cultivate Passion. As Duckworth writes:

> "Like it or not, there's a certain amount of trial and error inherent in the process of interest discovery. Unlike the answers to crossword puzzles, there isn't just one thing you can do that might develop into a passion. There are many. You don't have to find the "right" one, or even the "best" one — just a direction that feels good."[27]

This quote brings to mind the story of private equity entrepreneur and Twitter sensation Sahil Bloom. If you're at all familiar with Twitter these days, you're likely to know about Sahil Bloom. If not, you probably won't.

Prior to the COVID pandemic, Bloom spent his entire career in the private equity (PE) world, complete with its lucrative compensation packages and opportunities for advancement. He was making more and more money and feeling great about his future prospects. Things were good.

The problem was, like anyone working in PE, he barely had any time to even look up, regularly experiencing 80 to 100-hour work weeks.

When the pandemic hit, however, Bloom suddenly found extra time on his hands to think about more than just his work. For the prior year, he had been posting things here and there on Twitter, mostly just to satisfy his joy of writing. The thought of pursuing social media professionally never crossed his mind.

But there was something of an issue: he was good at it — really good. His insightful posts and keen insights began attracting more and more followers. When he started seeing some friends successfully leveraging their social media presence, he considered starting a little side hustle. Create an agency. Or some courses. Or even a newsletter.

So, he did.

Soon his followership was mushrooming. He was becoming something of a Twitter sensation, facing an interesting inflection point:

Should he stay in his nice, cushy job?

Should he pursue a different position with another PE firm, one that was actively recruiting him to come onboard?

Or should he leap into the unknown and go all in on a Twitter-based strategy?

On the verge of accepting the other PE role, a close friend asked why he would choose something he had minimal passion for when he'd discovered the thing that gave him energy, felt scalable, and fired him up.

Stopped dead in his tracks, Bloom knew what he really wanted to do. Exploring his curiosity and writing about what he learned along the way made him come alive. And the place to do it was on social media.

Today, Bloom has close to a million followers on Twitter (and growing daily), started his own investment fund, and has a very successful agency business and newsletter. None of this has come from some sort of prescribed passion that he was destined to follow. Instead, Bloom discovered his interest, found a direction that felt good, and is now using his joy of writing to create his own story of coming alive.

And those of us who follow him are inspired to come alive as well.

MY PASSION STORY

While my story looks different from Bloom's, it, too, followed a path of cultivating my interests. As I mentioned at the start of the book, I grew up in what would likely be called your typical middle-to-lower-middle-class home. Son of a City of Los Angeles street surveyor and his homemaker wife. House in the suburbs (Van Nuys, to be exact, to some the armpit of Southern California). One older brother. Two Volkswagens. Once-a-year camping vacation. And Little League. Lots of Little League.

When I was a kid, the first test I ever failed was when I was asked to name the four seasons, and I answered, "football, basketball, baseball, and hockey" (winter, spring, summer, and fall were not the officially recognized seasons in the house I grew up in). I thought for sure I would be a professional athlete of some sort.

Lack of skill and size put a quick end to that focused desire, but it didn't end my interest in teamwork.

After many years of being on teams of all sorts, most of them not in sports, I cultivated an even deeper interest in leading teams. Through trial and error, that deeper interest grew into a focus on finding ways to encourage others to live — really live. And that focus on encouraging others to really live ultimately led to the development of the Delta Theorem and to coaching and inspiring people toward the kind of elite living that says, "Everyone dies; not everyone really lives."

So, for me, people living at an elite level has always held my interest. Figuring out ways to encourage them to do so brings me intrinsic enjoyment. I am passionate about inspiring people to be alive. Whether in previous roles doing things like training subordinates to present effectively to a group of superiors or in my current role coaching people on purpose and performance, I am interested in seeing people fulfill their roles in the larger story we all find ourselves caught up in.

That's Passion for me. It came from a bit of discovery, followed by much development, and then a lifetime of deepening.

What's your Passion?

SHOW UP | ENGAGE | DO THE WORK

Take some time to answer the following:

1. What activities do I enjoy doing, even when not paid or rewarded for them?

2. What are the things I am most motivated to learn about or explore?

3. What are the things that I am most excited or enthusiastic about?

4. What are the things that I find most fulfilling or satisfying?

5. What are the things that I am most interested in?

6. What are the things that I feel most alive or most energized doing?

7. What would I be willing to work hard at or sacrifice for because they are so important to me?

CHAPTER 5

WHY Is the Point

"The two most important days in life are the day you were born and the day you discover the reason why."

— Mark Twain

LANGUAGE IS A REMARKABLE thing. It makes communication possible… or at least easier than it would otherwise be. And it shapes us in novel and often stirring ways. I frequently find this when coming across words from other languages, words for which there are no pure English translations.

Take the Danish word "hygge."

Hygge is that feeling we have when huddled around a blazing fire while freezing our tails off in the cold of winter. It's a sense of everyday togetherness, wholeness, and well-being, of doing life together in a down-to-earth, soul-stirring manner, making it easy to feel safe and warm, inside and out.

My wife creates hygge in our home, and I love it.

Or how about the German word "fisselig"? Fisselig describes being so flustered when we're in the presence of someone important that we become functionally incompetent. Think "first presentation in front of the boss." Palms get sweaty, eye sockets go cold, and we may even stutter and shake, sometimes having to be saved by a colleague.

Then there's the moment of hesitation just before introducing someone because we can't quite remember their name. The Scots call this a "tartle," that awkward moment where you can only hope the blank expression on your face doesn't betray your brain cramp.

My wife and I have developed a "tartle defense system" when we attend social gatherings. To avoid one of us becoming a turtle because of a tartle (slowly retreating into our shell when greeting someone), the other steps in and first introduces themselves to get the other person's name. Works every time when done naturally to avoid suspicion.

In the Delta Theorem, there's a similar translation idea when it comes to the concept of purpose. I call it Alpha.

THE MEANING OF ALPHA

Imagine having a conversation with a six-year-old that goes something like this:

"What are you doing?"
"Sending an email to my boss."
"Why?"
"Because I want to update her on the project I'm working on."
"Why?"
"Because I want her to feel informed."
"Why?"
"Because I would rather not get fired."

"Why?"
"Because we need money."
"Why?"

It's easy to see how patience gets tested in a conversation like this. Persistent questioning can be annoying. But it can also be instructive.

Digging deeper and deeper with persistent 'why's' often unearths significant motivators, revealing a lot about purpose. It also confronts us with questions as to what our motivators should be. Reasons we have for actions we take — in this case, being motivated by financial security — get revealed.

In the Delta Theorem, "Alpha" translates as the ultimate answer to the most profound question of "Why?"

Symbolic of its place as the first letter in the Greek alphabet, Alpha represents our primary or first purpose, our powerful WHY. It's what Simon Sinek refers to as a deep-seated cause or belief that is the source of our motivation and inspiration. It's also what Frederick Buechner describes as "the place where our deep gladness meets the world's deep need."

(Pause for a moment to think about that: The place where our deep gladness meets the world's deep need. Wow! That is indeed powerful.)

> With a powerful WHY as the source of our intention, we find ourselves in the best position to make spontaneous and appropriate decisions for the actions we take in our lives.

Alpha is the harmony of our Priorities, Principles, and Passion (P^3), or as Bill Plotkin puts it in his book, *Soulcraft*, "what is genuinely yours to offer the world before you can make it a better place… your unique gift to bring to your community. The most you can do to love and serve the world is to offer that gift — your true self. And it is all the world needs."[28]

We are bombarded by so much noise; so many voices tell us how we should think or what to do. Alpha is the place where our P^3 quiets the noise. Where the integration of each of the P^3 aspects is intentional, allowing for control — not control over others, but control over one's own direction, choice, and decision.

With a powerful WHY as the source of our intention, we find ourselves in the best position to make spontaneous and appropriate decisions for the actions we take in our lives.

THE ALPHA LASER

To understand what is meant by the harmony of P^3, start by visualizing the individual elements of our Priorities, Principles, and Passion as three independent circles, each interlocking into areas of overlap, similar to that of the Olympic Rings.

I use the graphic below to illustrate the point:

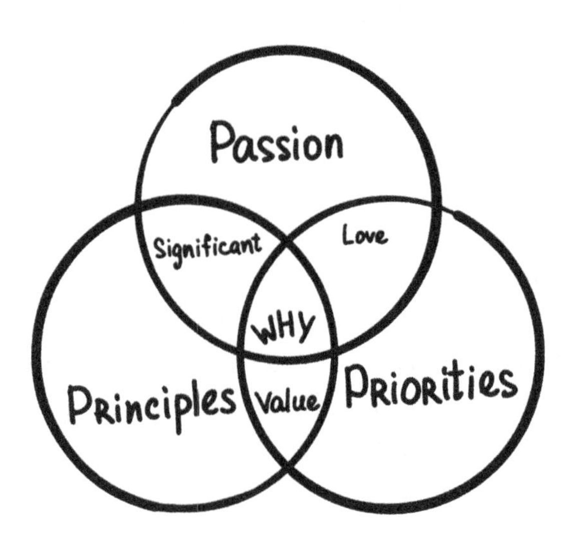

Passion Plus Principles

Where Passion overlaps with Principles, we find things that hold particular significance in our lives — the things that have a high level of influence on us.

For instance, I have a Passion for sport, and a Principle I strive to live by is "Seek the Uncommon." So, the overlap I see is risk. Sport requires putting oneself on the line, and to do it in an uncommon way, one must have the courage to risk. I recognize that risk, then, as something significant to me.

Passion Plus Priorities

Similarly, where Passion and Priorities overlap, we find things we love. More significant than mere enthusiasm, these form deep-rooted and long-lasting attachments. They are the focus of our desires.

So, continuing with my story, my Passion for sport overlaps with the high importance I place on health and fitness into what I interpret as aliveness. Sport gets my competitive juices flowing; health and fitness get me active. Feeling fully alive is what I love and am deeply attached to.

Principles Plus Priorities

And finally, where Principles and Priorities overlap, we find what we value — those standards of behavior we attach importance to because of their substance or usefulness.

Again, taking my example, when combining my willingness to risk with a Priority of health and fitness, I uncovered that I value excellence. To risk is to expose oneself to potential danger, while health and fitness often involve activities that stretch us, so I see the overlap as pursuing excellence.

Notice I didn't say pursuing perfection. Excellence is striving to live at an elite level, above mediocrity, or what the ancient Greeks called *arete* — a term describing maximum ability and potency for action, effectiveness, and skill in goodness. It doesn't eliminate the chance of failure. Perfection is being free from any flaws or failure — a big difference.

Passion, Principles, and Priorities: The Alpha Laser

None of the areas of overlap among two of the P^3 group in and of itself represents a primary purpose. It is only where all the circles intersect that we find our powerful WHY, our Alpha, forming the source of motivation for how we act daily.

It's like the executive, legislative, and judicial branches of the U.S. government, where no one branch is meant to be more powerful than the others. Our Priorities, Principles, and Passion counterbalance each other to uncover our deep gladness, our true selves.

I like to think of it as the energy of light. When diffused and spread out, it has very little force. When concentrated and intense like a laser, however, it can slice through almost anything, even metal.

For me, my Alpha laser is **to inspire aliveness, to live at an elite level while encouraging others to do the same**. It's a statement that's unique to me and my current situation and encompasses risk, aliveness, and excellence. It provides my life with meaning.

ALPHA IN ACTION

Another example is my client, Paul. In his mid-40s, Paul is a successful software business developer and side-hustle entrepreneur, happily married with three kids. When I started coaching him, he described himself as driven and on a mission but couldn't define what he was driven toward or what mission he was on.

At the time, Paul was passionate about his wife and kids, endurance competitions, being a top salesperson, and remaining present and grateful. He held firmly to the principle of Kaizen (continuous improvement) and was committed to "Walk the Walk" as a personal mantra. The focus of his desire was to be present, positive, creative, spiritual, active, and true to himself.

Paul identified his top Priorities as his Spousal Relationship ("Spend more time with my wife with no limits"), Extended Family ("Be a teacher and role model to my three kids" and "Support my mom financially"), and a combination of Career/Wealth ("Become an active angel investor/start-up incubator").

When we started unearthing his Priorities, Principles, and Passion, what began to emerge was a powerful WHY for how he wanted to show up and engage in life. He began to recognize that some of the things he had been conditioned to believe he was *supposed to* do — in his words, "Go to college, build a career, family, enjoy and be grateful for what I have, and play it safe" — did not bring life.

Instead, Paul saw his purpose as: "Be the best version of myself, so I can raise three amazing kids who will lead, create, and thrive in this world."

Paul's drive became the pursuit of having an inscription on his tombstone to one day read, "Just whisper my name in your heart, and I will be there." He was now on a mission to take "responsibility during my time on earth to contribute in a meaningful way and endeavor to do my part and make this amazing place a little better than when I arrived."

He took control of his life by seeing how he could be intentional.

I have witnessed Paul live out his powerful WHY, and the results have been inspiring. Rather than stay safe in a cushy but spiritless job, he pursued and landed a business development position with a cutting-edge tech company that had one of the most successful IPOs in recent years. He engages his kids in endurance crucibles he plans and participates in, where they come together as a family and build their physical, mental, and emotional intelligence in the process.

Finally, and perhaps most importantly, Paul is walking beside his wife as she experiences some significant health challenges. When Paul's name is whispered... or called out... he is there.

Many may fall into the trap of thinking that a powerful WHY needs to be something profound and remarkable. It doesn't. The only thing it has to be is profoundly personal, just like mine is for me, and Paul's is for him.

IKIGAI – THE REASON FOR BEING

What I have been describing is what the Japanese call *ikigai*. In Japanese, *iki* means life, and *gai* means worth. Thus, ikigai refers to that which gives life worth. It's more dynamic than simply finding purpose. It's the reason for being, the synergistic harmony of your P^3 into a powerful WHY.

Consider some essential qualities of an ikigai:

- It's challenging: Ikigai leads to mastery and growth.
- It's individual: Pursuing an ikigai involves autonomy, freedom, and choice.
- It's engaging: Ikigai involves commitments of time and enthusiasm, often to a particular cause, skill, trade, or group of people.
- It's positive: Ikigai boosts well-being, creating more energy than one uses.

In the same way, your Alpha is challenging, individual, engaging, and positive. It is your reason for being.

I love the story of Milada Horáková, a Czech politician elected to Parliament before the communist coup in February 1948, to illustrate Alpha and ikigai.

Despite being urged by friends to leave Czechoslovakia, Horáková remained politically active in the country, refusing to accept the legality of the communist government. The authorities arrested her, charged her with conspiracy against the state, and sentenced her to death. Refusing to accept clemency in exchange for a confession, Horáková was ultimately executed by hanging.

The night before her execution, Horáková wrote a letter to her sixteen-year-old daughter. In it, she wrote the following:

> "The reason was not that I loved you little; I love you just as purely and fervently as other mothers love their children. But I understood that my task here in the world was to do you good… by seeing to it that life becomes better, and that all children can live well. Don't be frightened and sad because I am not coming back anymore. Learn, my child, to look at life early as a serious matter. Life is hard, it does not pamper anybody, and every time it strokes you it gives you ten blows. Become accustomed to that soon, but don't let it defeat you. Decide to fight."[29]

It's easy to get a glimpse of Horáková's convicting Priorities, the Principles upon which she stood, and the Passion by which she lived. And ultimately, we get to appreciate her ikigai, her reason for being, her powerful WHY.

Horáková found purpose in doing good "by seeing to it that life becomes better and that all children can live well." Her deep gladness, even in sadness, met the world's deep need.

While Milada Horáková leaves us with what seems like a grand and extraordinary Alpha, she's more the exception than the norm. My client Paul's powerful WHY had just as much impact on his world as Horáková's. Ours can, too.

Unfortunately, what is more than the norm, though, is living life devoid of any understanding of WHY at all. Or, even more devastatingly, living in and through circumstances that make pursuing purpose nearly impossible. We go day to day just surviving and existing. We must consider that next.

PURPOSE AND THE HIERARCHY OF NEEDS

In 1943, psychologist Abraham Maslow created the Hierarchy of Needs[30]; the idea being that we as humans cannot move on to bigger and better things until our most basic needs are met.

For example, we can't focus on becoming wealthy if we can't pay for food or our rent; we aren't able to concentrate on anything besides having a safe place to sleep at night.

What does this have to do with purpose? The answer is simple: it's naive and disingenuous to discuss finding our purpose if we don't acknowledge that there are times and situations when our most basic needs can't be met. And that includes having stable mental health. It's only when basic needs are met and we are stable mentally that we can even begin to focus on finding our purpose.

Let's look at Maslow's hierarchy to see what I mean.

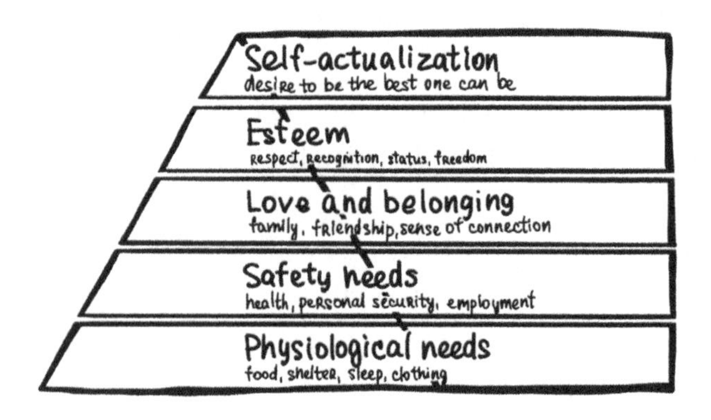

The first level of Maslow's hierarchy is physiological needs. These are the most basic human needs. Air, water, food, shelter, sleep, etc. If these needs are not met, let's face it, there's no way you can focus on anything else. You are in survivor mode, and your body will do whatever it must to simply stay alive, even such drastic measures as shutting down critical functioning such as mental health to preserve energy as necessary. You may give up your freedom and self-respect to survive. To speak of ikigais and powerful WHYs at this level is almost cruel.

The second level is safety needs. These are the needs that protect your survival, including personal security, financial well-being, and physical resources, often manifested through finding and maintaining employment or having access to good medical care. Powerful WHYs start to become more important at this level, but it's still challenging to emphasize their full development.

The third level is love and belonging. This is where you need to feel a sense of connection, to feel loved and accepted by others — family, friends, and community. At this stage, having a sense of purpose starts to become more and more significant.

The fourth level is esteem, where you have to feel good about yourself — confident, respected, competent, and valuable. Achievements, accomplishments, and recognition meet this need. Often, the benefits of esteem are a direct result of living out your powerful WHY.

The fifth and final level is self-actualization. This is when you reach your full potential, actually fulfilling your purpose. You are motivated by personal growth and development.

The takeaway is to acknowledge that people need to have their physiological and safety needs met before they can even begin to think about finding their purpose.

In other words, you must crawl before you can run.

Once you have met your most basic needs, you can then begin to focus on exploring Alpha. Even still, while having a definitive sense of Purpose may be a luxury not all can have, it is still something you can work towards. But, like Passion, it's a process of cultivation.

CULTIVATING OUR PURPOSE

Unless you are drawn to your WHY through some social or cultural prescription or have experienced some life-altering event that pulls you, there is no magic bullet — it takes time. So, you have to experiment and see what you are drawn to.

You don't know what you don't know, and you can't see what you like or don't like if you don't experiment with new things. In addition, Purpose, like Priorities and Passion, evolves over time, becoming a living thing in and of itself.

For instance, when you are young, you will spend more time trying to land a career, start a business, or build a family. Through trial and error, you will begin to form opinions about what you are willing to do and not do. Over time, you build resistance or admiration toward concepts, activities, and people. As you age, you refine your Priorities and discover new Passions. Your needs and wants shift. You will shed what doesn't work and lean into what does.

Often, Purpose can be elusive. You can't depend on it just showing up one day. It may reveal itself when you aren't looking for it. That is why I often use the phrase "find your Purpose." But there are two ways to find something. You can do it through actively looking (cultivating) or by happenstance.

Often, Purpose can be elusive. You can't depend on it just showing up one day. It may reveal itself when you aren't looking for it.

Purpose Is a Journey

Cultivating Purpose focuses on the journey rather than landing at a destination. An excellent way to do this is using the Odyssey Plan, a tool created by Stanford professors Bill Burnet and Dave Evans.[31] It combines instinct and intuition with rational thinking to explore different paths to our WHY.

Start with the version of a potential WHY from work done on harmonizing P^3. Next, assess it under three different scenarios:

- How well does it reflect your current path?
- How might it be different if money didn't matter?
- How might it be different if other people's expectations didn't matter?

Rank each scenario based on the following:

- How well does this fit with your Priorities, Principles, and Passion?
- How much confidence do you have in it?
- How much does it make you come alive?

The bottom line is that when you work to cultivate Purpose, you must dig beyond your likes and dislikes, strengths and weaknesses. It requires commitment.

COMMITTED TO PURPOSE

One thing I can almost always count on in my coaching is the baffled look that my clients get if I ask, "What's your purpose?" They don't need convincing that it's essential to know their purpose, but it's such a big concept to get their arms around that they usually respond with, "I have no idea!"

In addition, there's the problem of "optionality."

If you state your purpose, does that mean you no longer have the option for it to be something else? It's just much more comfortable to have an "either/or" or a "this then that" approach: "I'm hoping to inspire others to be free or maybe to inspire aliveness;" "I might start by taking a risk with my job and eventually make my life about adventure."

When blended, all of this causes you to default not just to the "I have no idea" but to an "It's just too much to take up" mindset.

But it really isn't too much. We've already seen how breaking down purpose into its more digestible elements of P^3 can lead you into cultivation and discovery, so it's doable if you take it in bite-size chunks. As you take the time to identify and diagram your P^3, you slow down, focus, and center your thoughts.

And when you center, you become intentional, creating a positive cycle of thinking and feeling that aligns with your true self. The payoff is too great to ignore.

Multiple studies have shown that those with a sense of purpose, who know their powerful WHY, have better physical and mental health and lower mortality rates. They are more balanced and even-keeled. They have perseverance and grit.

Research has also shown that having a sense of purpose is a good predictor of higher income and net worth. So, knowing your WHY is vital. Your future can literally depend on it.

LIVING OUR WHY

The sweetener to discovering your powerful WHY is in living it out. Like anything, it doesn't happen through contemplation alone. You have to commit to consistent action, making adjustments along the way. You do that by being intentional.

You decide where and how your life goes. You choose who and what you want to be.

When you develop an attitude to live each day with purpose, on purpose, you intentionally inject that meaning into everything you do. You make every moment and every activity meaningful, and you help others do the same in their own lives and in the lives of their loved ones.

You often find your powerful WHY by connecting with those around you. You establish a shared purpose and understanding of what matters to you through relationships.

Being in community allows you to learn from each other, offer emotional and practical support, and create a safe space for exploration and growth. You can ask for help or advice and be there for others when they need you. In this way, you can create meaningful connections that feed into your personal journey of discovery.

You have to be ready and willing to take action to live out your purpose. More than purpose, though, you also need realism.

Where do you start? What do you do first? What do you do right now? How are you convinced that what you're doing is moving you forward?

That's what Effort is all about, and it's where we turn next after a short exercise.

SHOW UP | ENGAGE | DO THE WORK

Take some time to answer the following:

1. What are the things that bring you the most joy and fulfillment in your life?

2. What are your strengths and talents, and how can you use them to impact the world positively?

3. What are your long-term goals and aspirations?

4. What are the causes or issues that you are most concerned about?

5. What things do you wish to change or improve in the world?

6. How do you want to be remembered by others after you're gone?

7. What is your ideal vision of your life, and how can you work toward making it a reality?

CHAPTER 6

Effort: The Accelerant

"It is not uncommon for people to spend their whole life waiting to start living."
— Eckhart Tolle

IN 2019, MIT professor Abhijit Banerjee and two colleagues won the Nobel Prize in Economics for their experimental approach to reducing global poverty. It was an honor Banerjee had never thought possible. Early in his academic career, he was caught up in the herd mentality of academia, holding that theory reigned supreme over actual outcomes. Like the architect who outlines an optimal structure on paper, good theories outline optimal solutions to any problem.

Develop a theory and have your solution. Or so the thinking went.

But something didn't sit quite right for Banerjee. While economists provided their theories, he was troubled that what these economists —many world-renowned — were coming up with were just stories, failing to appropriately connect the dots on the causes and consequences of poverty. So instead, Banerjee used real-life actions to discover what did and didn't work. He went to rural villages and put together randomized trials, similar to clinical studies in medical research, to measure the effectiveness of economic programs. He wanted to know how things worked in reality, not just theoretically.

Banerjee was interested in the difference between theory and practice. And when it comes to the Delta Theorem, so am I.

DIFFERENCE BETWEEN THEORY AND PRACTICE

Author and executive John Mariotti said, "In theory there is very little difference between theory and practice; in practice there's a hell of a lot of difference." Theory assumes an outcome. Practice tests theory to see if it is accurate.

As a Papua New Guinea proverb puts it: "Knowledge is only a rumor until it lives in the muscle."

That's what we're after when discussing Effort in relation to the Delta Theorem. It's taking the theory of Alpha and P^3 ("knowledge is rumor") and bringing it to life through action ("lives in the muscle"). Taking concept and putting it into practice. Converting purpose into performance.

More than just knowledge and understanding, using and living by the Delta Theorem requires discipline, commitment, and hard work. It requires intentional and sustained Effort, the kind of Effort that creates momentum to get things moving. Momentum similar in concept to that found in the Laws of Motion.

EFFORT AND THE LAWS OF MOTION

The Laws of Motion state that things at rest will remain at rest unless acted upon by an external force. When force is applied, movement happens.

In layperson's terms, if something is sitting still, it will continue to sit still unless something comes along and slams into it. Then it will move.

Think cue ball moving toward an eight ball as a result of being struck by the cue stick in your hand. It's Newton's Second Law of Motion: $F = ma$, not just a logo on tee shirts and coffee mugs where it seems to show up mostly these days.

In the Delta Theorem, Effort is the accelerant that slams into your reason for being, creating motion and momentum. It has a multiplier effect, creating an exponentially larger impact on your world as a direct result.

It's similar in concept to the approach Khe Hy developed regarding prioritizing. You may recall from our look at Priorities how Hy illustrated an issue using the Eisenhower Method for prioritizing. We often identify most of our actions and efforts as Important and Urgent, causing too many to be Priorities and us needing help with all of them.

Hy's alternative solution evaluates actions and efforts through a model that uses "What Moves the Needle" as its criterion. More specifically, what moves a financial needle, at least conceptually?

For instance, perhaps you evaluate checking email as busy work that amounts to $10 per hour of value for you. That would make sense since that's less than the minimum wage in more than half of the states in the U.S. If it's all you did with your days, you would not be able to survive, rendering it true busy work. Hy suggests you ask yourself this question: What's 1000 times more impactful than checking email? In other words, what are efforts you make that are worth $10,000/hour instead of $10/hour? Once you do that, you prioritize the $10,000/hour efforts instead of the $10/hour ones.

According to Hy, these efforts take high skill and create high leverage. (For more on Hy's model, check out "The Magic of Doing $10,000 per Hour Work."[32])

But let's face it, none of this matters if you don't get moving in the first place. And to do that, we look at the one demand I make of all my clients: Show Up — Engage — Do the Work. (OK, it's three things, but I see them as one!)

SHOW UP

According to Austrian psychologist and holocaust survivor Viktor Frankl, between stimulus and response, there is a space. In that space is your power to choose a response. For however brief or prolonged that space lasts, it is an opportunity to decide how to respond. How to show up.

In relation to the Delta Theorem, it's considered a moment of "respond-ability" or responding with responsibility. It's having an attitude that says there's no time like the present. No need to put off to tomorrow what we can do today.

If we wait for the right time to show up, we may be waiting forever.

> If we wait for the right time to show up, we may be waiting forever.

Take, for instance, a common interaction I have with my wife. She comes home and finds me writing away, trying like mad to finish this book. She looks at me and asks, "Can you do the dishes in the sink?"

For a brief moment, I have a choice for how to respond. I can be receptive and helpful, responding with "Sure, no worries, I know it's important to you, let me go ahead and finish what I'm doing and get them done," or I can be snarky and defensive, responding with "I hate it when you come home and find something to put me to work on, knowing full well I'm busy." In either case, my "respond-ability" is at stake.

No one has gotten this better than the global athletic apparel brand Nike. In rolling out its brilliant marketing slogan, *Just Do It*, Nike saw "respond-ability" as taking action. Putting in the effort. Not making excuses.

With *Just Do It*, Nike gave us all permission to show up. It's what has made it such a brilliant slogan, one of the best crafted concerning effort.

But it's not just about *whether* we show up. With Nike, as with the Delta Theorem, it's about being relentless when we do.

Being Relentless

According to Tim Grover, author and former trainer of Michael Jordan and Kobe Bryant, being relentless is about never being satisfied. In *Relentless: From Good to Great to Unstoppable*[33], Grover emphasizes that success is a journey, not a destination. It's not enough to simply reach a goal; you must continue to push yourself to make progress and grow. It's having a "never give up" attitude while creating new goals whenever you reach your best.

If you're good, you don't stop until you're great. If you're great, you fight until you're unstoppable.

Grover describes three different ways to show up: as a Cooler, as a Closer, or as a Cleaner. He writes:

> A Cooler is careful; they wait to be told what to do, watch to see what everyone else is doing, and then follow the leader.
>
> A Closer can handle much pressure; they'll get the job done if you put them in the right situation and tell them precisely what you need them to do.

> Cleaners don't just do a job; they define the job. They take responsibility for everything. When something goes wrong, they don't blame others. Instead, they clean up the mess and move on.[34]

Cleaners are the ones who will push the boundaries and take the initiative. They don't simply wait for instructions; they proactively seek the next challenge or goal. They are never content with the status quo and strive to be constantly improving.

Just take a look at some of the comparisons Grover gives of the three:

Coolers	Closers	Cleaners
Have an amazing game	Have an amazing season	Have amazing careers
Worry about the competition	Study the competition	Make the competition study them
Won't offer to take on a role they're not comfortable with	Will take the role if you ask them, and they'll do it well	Don't wait to be asked; they just do it

Obviously, not everyone is or can be a Cleaner. But no matter which type you are, one thing is certain: you've got to show up. And once you do, you're ready for the next step when it comes to Effort: You Engage.

ENGAGE

Wouldn't it be wonderful if all your actions could be done on autopilot? Life would be so much easier. And wouldn't it be great if you could make painful and uncomfortable actions effortless, especially those you know are good for you? All your most dreaded actions — ones like working out, eating healthy, saving for retirement — would just happen.

Unfortunately, you can't.

Action never happens on its own. It's never effortless. It demands active participation and involvement. It requires energy.

Action never happens on its own. It's never effortless. It demands active participation and involvement. It requires energy.

Action requires engagement. It is being an active participant or contributor. Rather than simply observing or remaining passive, it means taking the initiative, getting involved, fostering creativity, and collaborating with others.

While engagement is effortful, there is a way to make Effort *feel* effortless. That way is known as the state of flow.

Effortless Effort

According to Mihaly Csikszentmihalyi, the Hungarian psychologist who coined the term, you enter a state of flow when you experience focused, intense concentration. It's a deeply personal space where your mind is still — to the point of effortlessness. You are fully engaged, tuning out the noise and focusing solely on the actions at hand.

Many call it being "in the zone," the place where your thinking is deliberate and focused. It's just you and your gut energized to the maximum.

In the flow state, you are entirely engaged and devoted to the activity at hand. You become almost unaware of your thoughts and instead focus on the action itself. You may find yourself in a state of heightened awareness, where your senses are more acute, and your decision-making is more instinctive.

Consider this example from Lance P. Hickey, Ph.D.:

> You are skiing down a mountain trail in Aspen — one of the expert diamond slopes. Though you have skied down this slope before, you have never been able to "dominate" it — until now. You begin to hit your stride, striking every mogul perfectly, effortlessly. Your actions seem frozen in time, and every little sound becomes more intense — the crisp slap of your skis against the powder, the scrunch of your knees, and your rhythmic breathing. You might even describe yourself as having become "one with the mountain." All those years of training and struggling, taking ski lessons, and tumbling into the woods, are now finally justified. You have had, quite literally, a peak experience.[35]

All we can say is, "Ahhh…."

This is consistent with a well-known model called the Four Stages of Competence.

The Four Stages of Competence

In the Four Stages of Competence, there's a progression of psychological states that move from total incompetence to complete competence. When it comes to the learning and development of any ability or concept, it breaks down like this:

- Initially, we are unaware of how little we know (unconscious incompetence).

- As we recognize our incompetence, we begin to develop and acquire an ability or skill consciously, but we still bumble and fumble in it (conscious incompetence).
- Then, we consciously use it in a way that is more effective and useful (conscious competence).
- Eventually, the ability is being used effectively and almost naturally without being consciously thought through (unconscious competence).

Along a similar line, French philosopher Pascal Engel proposed something like the stages of incompetence by classifying stupidity into various levels or degrees, starting at the lowest stage of the dull-witted and moronic (those whose intelligence is so low that it approaches that of animals), and progressing upward toward that of the sophisticated fool (those who have a form of moral defect, often ignoring and despising moral values, willing to say almost anything without worrying whether it's true or false). When overlaying both models, we get something like this:

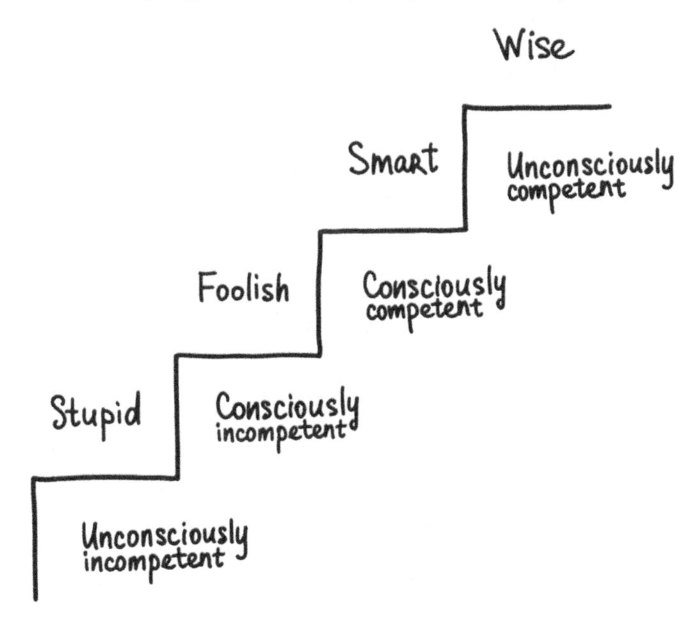

As can be seen in the diagram, being in that place where we are unconsciously competent — where it's not just smarts but wisdom — is when we are "in the zone."

It's pretty easy to see how "in the zone" can make any action feel effortless. But how do you do this? How do you take actions… and maybe even more specifically, dreaded actions… and make them feel like no action at all?

The best way I know is by turning actions into habits. But to do this, you first start with creating rituals.

Creating Flow Through Rituals

Similar to habits, only better, rituals are often seen as more meaningful or significant than habits. For example, rituals break down large, seemingly insurmountable actions into smaller, more achievable ones.

Rituals are typically done with greater intention, creating a sense of the mythical, almost spiritual, with them, and are particularly helpful with actions that require motivation and focus.

When following rituals, you create comfort and structure in times of uncertainty. Because they come from a high level of energy and consciousness, you are fully engaged, focusing on the experience of the actions rather than just their completion. That's different from following a routine. With routine, you also follow a regular sequence of actions but without the same sense of purpose.

Similarly, rituals differ from habits concerning the level of energy and consciousness involved. But once you consistently establish a ritual, it soon becomes a routine, requiring less energy and consciousness. Not long after, it transforms into habit, requiring very little energy and consciousness.

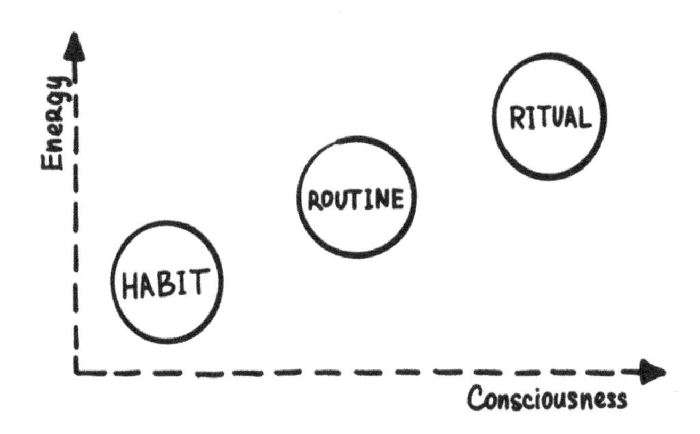

It's like creating muscle/motor memory.

Say you're learning to play an instrument and create a ritual that includes practicing for one hour daily. Your body recalls what you have learned, making it hard to forget. It relies on repeating the ritual over an extended period to "store" the coordination in memory.

The more you follow the ritual, the easier the playing of the instrument becomes. With time and consistency, the effortful action becomes effortless. As a result, the ritual turns into a routine, and then, a habit.

It is what former BlackRock portfolio manager and founder of the Ship 30 for 30 online writing course Dickie Bush and his partner Nicolas Cole have coined a "daily date" with yourself. They call them "Sacred Hours," blocked-off chunks of time with no distractions and no responsibilities.

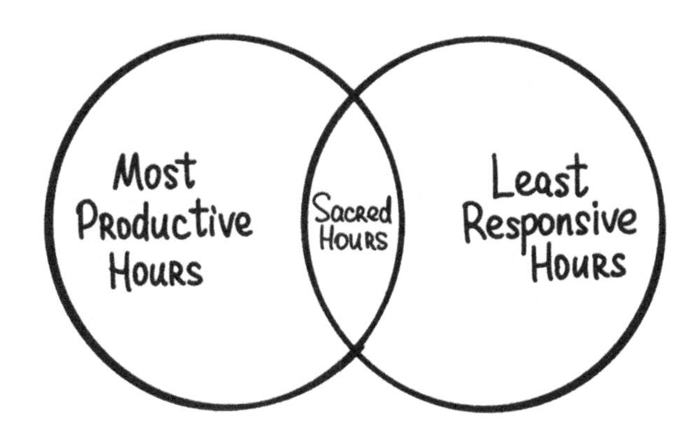

According to Bush and Cole, Sacred Hours is a consistent time of day where our most productive time intersects with our least responsive time. They're unique for each of us, but once we've discovered the optimal intersection, we block it out and make it a time of ritual.

To help get days started right, I encourage my clients to develop a Morning Ritual — regularly followed actions done first thing in the morning to kick-start the day. My Morning Ritual looks something like this:

- Set the alarm to wake up at or near the same time each morning. (Body clock often makes setting the alarm unnecessary these days.)
- Drink a glass of water.
- Read several daily devotionals.
- Do breathing exercises, mixing in meditation/prayer/visualization while balancing on a wobble cushion in front of a Joov red light therapy panel.
- Take my Golden Retriever out for a walk or run, incorporating some weight (vest and/or wrist) resistance.
- Complete some body-weight exercises.
- Sit in my one-person infrared sauna.
- Get some free cryotherapy by taking a cold shower or a pool plunge.

Having followed this ritual consistently for several years, I've noticed all activities have become second nature to me. I don't even think about them anymore. They're now habits, tied closely with my powerful WHY.

Depending on the circumstances, I may not get to everything every day, but on the days that I don't, I definitely feel exposed and almost vulnerable. That's the mystical power of ritual.

(Personally, I find it hard to come up with actions that I can use to create a ritual. To help with this, I compiled a list of 100 actions to spur imagination. It can be found in the APPENDIX.)

Keeping Ritual Alive and Well

Fortunately or unfortunately, being human means we're attracted to novelty, growing discontented with the same old, same old. We may love the power of habit, but the idea of ritual might turn us off because of the villain it's partnered with: Boredom.

What's the key to avoiding boredom? Spontaneity. And the key to spontaneity? Creativity.

So how can you be spontaneous when it comes to rituals?

Consider the following:

Pull the Grenade Pin: Set a timer and make a ritual feel like a race against time… which turns it into a game… which makes it exciting.

Have a Hoedown: Build in some music to generate energy during the ritual; there's nothing like some boogie to keep the groove in life.

Give It a Tip of the Hat: Reflect with gratefulness on having the ability to do what you're doing during the ritual; all power to act is worth celebrating.

Mise en Place (MEEZ ahn plahs): Set up the environment to make it easy to get things done; outfit it with proper tools or ingredients (like a great French chef, thus the fancy tag); declutter unnecessary items.

Start Fresh: Use an existing ritual's disruption (for instance, you tweak your knee and need to modify your workout ritual) as an opportunity to create a new ritual or to add a further action to a current ritual.

Reframe: Choose to see things differently; instead of "I have to," think, "I get to"; instead of "I can't," think, "I don't"; tap into the powerful WHY.

OK Is Good Enough: Periodically be flexible and lower your standards, accepting that you're not letting yourself down but being reasonable.

Make a Mini: Experiment with mini rituals — tiny, positive actions that you force yourself to do — whose "too small to fail" nature makes them easy to play with. For instance, say you want to get up earlier to fit in exercise. Start by setting the alarm ten minutes earlier every week. If you currently rise at 8 a.m. and want to get to 7 a.m., start with 7:50 a.m. for the first week, then go back ten more minutes to 7:40 a.m. for the second week. After a mere month and a half, you'll be at your 7 a.m. target.

I love how Brené Brown puts it in her book *Rising Strong*: "Creativity embeds knowledge so that it can become practice. We move what we're learning from our heads to our hearts through our hands. We are born makers, and creativity is the ultimate act of integration — it is how we fold our experiences into our being."[36]

OK. So, we've shown up and engaged. Now it's now time to do the work.

DO THE WORK

There's actually a law, Zipf's Law, that says that when we are given several different options, we will select the option that takes the least effort.[37] Just like water, we seek the path of least resistance.

Resonates, doesn't it? We tend to be lazy, looking for the easiest way to get by. It's the reason for emphasizing doing the work when considering Effort in the Delta Theorem.

No Pain, No Gain

To Do the Work means taking purposeful action, getting outside your comfort zone, and doing things that demand near-maximal Effort beyond your current abilities. While you may hate it, being outside your comfort zone becomes the key to your growth and long-term contentment. Just consider the work of Michael Easter from his book, *The Comfort Crisis*.[38]

While you may hate it, being outside your comfort zone becomes the key to your growth and long-term contentment.

In his research, Easter discovered that living outside your comfort zone improves your health and happiness dramatically. Your willingness to take on challenges unlocks creative energies you could not access.

Easter's findings make a strong case for pushing yourself beyond your comfort zone. Creating new experiences allows you to explore your capabilities and reach your full potential. You can also develop a greater appreciation for life and the people around you.

But while this may sound inspiring on paper, let's face it: It's hard to think anyone would voluntarily invite pain into their lives. Why would they? Pain and discomfort typically serve as signals to stop whatever it is that's causing such pain.

Just think of any physical pain you experience. When you feel physical pain, your body is telling you to stop. You're injured. And yet, there's something about overcoming pain that you know is good for you. Your own experience bears this out, right?

Just think of the times that stick out the most to you regarding your growth. Were they times when everything was going well and life was humming? Or were they times you faced down the most difficult of circumstances?

I'd bet a nickel against a dollar that it is the latter. The best moments usually occur when you are stretched to your limits. It's something the Japanese have a practice surrounding. They call it the practice of *misogi.*

Misogi Training

Taken from an ancient Japanese religious ritual, a misogi represents a challenge to stretch your sense of what's possible. It's about putting yourself to the test under demanding circumstances.

Excuses have to be dropped. The mind has to focus. Performance peaks, change takes place, and you can endure almost anything, good or bad, that comes your way.

It's a practice of self-awareness and intentional growth.

Misogi has a rhythm to it: Pain first, pay-off later. It's pushing the boundary of what's possible and making an extraordinary effort, understanding that extraordinary results follow when extraordinary effort becomes commonplace.

Through engaging in misogi, you become more aware of your strengths and weaknesses and better understand how to use them to your advantage. As a result, you gain a greater understanding of your thoughts and beliefs, allowing you to approach life with an open mind and a willingness to learn.

In my case, it was a crucible like the one I endured when earning my coaching certification — 12 hours of Navy-SEAL-style drills to put me to the test. Succeed or fail was not the point. Pushing the boundary of what I thought possible was.

It was the essence of what it means to do the work when it comes to Effort in the Delta Theorem.

So far in this chapter, we have focused on describing Effort: its role as an accelerant, how to Show Up, how to Engage, and how to Do the Work. Now I want to introduce the target of our Effort: Integrated Wholeness.

THE SIX FACETS FRAMEWORK

As humans, we possess many competencies, all of which work together in an integrated manner to create our overall sense of wholeness. By competencies, I mean the skills, abilities, and knowledge necessary to live wholeheartedly. They include cognitive abilities, physical skills, gut sense, emotional intelligence, creativity, and spirituality. Each of these is a vital part of our identity and development.

A way to picture this is to consider a Rubik's Cube, complete with its six sides or facets, each of a different color and each consisting of nine different tiles.

First, consider each side or facet representative of the six competencies essential to our overall well-being. They include:

Spiritual (white facet) – Our innermost beliefs and values, including the sense of connection to something greater than ourselves.

Physical (blue facet) – Our biological systems, including such things as strength, endurance, appearance, and health.

Instinctual (yellow facet) – Our intuitional behaviors or responses, including pattern recognition and gut sense.

Natural (orange facet) – Our innate and even genetic qualities or tendencies, including temperament or personality.

Emotional (red facet) – Our psychological state, including thoughts, feelings, and degrees of pleasure or displeasure.

Mental (green facet) – Our cognitive skills, including logical reasoning, problem-solving, and learning.

In a standard cube, each of the facets consists of nine individual tiles. A way to think about that is that each competency has several attributes. For instance, attributes of physical competency might be stamina, speed, hydration, fueling, flexibility, and rest, whereas emotional competency might be mood, passions, self-regulation, impulse, and affection. The point is that each of the competencies consists of actual attributes. When put all together, this is what I call the Six Facets. It's the multifaceted, multidimensional concept that while each competency is essential for well-being, all must integrate for wholeness.

FROM WELLNESS TO WHOLENESS

In my coaching, I use the acronym SPIN-EM when considering the dynamic nature of the Six Facets. The tiles of our Six Facets are constantly spinning, forming different combinations. Unlike a Rubik's Cube, where the object is to spin the cube to solve for each side, with the Six Facets, we recognize that each of the competencies impacts each other, so the object is to be aware of the combination of different-colored tiles at any point in time so that we can blend them into an integrated whole. To do this, we must constantly challenge ourselves to learn new skills and practice old skills.

While it is simply impossible to master all of our competencies, it is possible to unlock greater potential by focusing on more than just one. By strengthening competencies that are underdeveloped but important while appreciating competencies that are strengths, you grow faster and are more balanced.

(A key way to do this is to create a Six Facets development plan. To learn more about a Six Facets development plan, visit www.rudiusstrategiesgroup.com)

JUST SCRATCHING THE SURFACE

I'm going to be a bit vulnerable here by saying that this chapter is far and away the most challenging write. And it's not because it was a misogi for me. It's because of the sheer volume of material that can be covered. So, while I did my best to focus on areas that I found most helpful, there are many left out.

For instance, we didn't get a chance to touch on discipline, willpower, or procrastination. I didn't address grit and perseverance nor learned helplessness and hope. There are external and internal motivations, triggers, and expectations that I couldn't cover, nor the tyranny of convenience. All of these additional areas, and others, have an impact on Effort.

So, as I do with my clients, I will do now. Don't stop here. Pick up books on grit by Angela Duckworth or Brad Ritter. Review the studies on learned helplessness that Martin Seligman and Steven

Maier conducted. Or the Harvard study on the power of hope using rats that swam. Listen to Piers Steel's book on procrastination. Just do something.

But also keep in mind: no matter how much we read or learn, nothing will give us success in making an impact unless we take action. We can't become trapped in theory trying to get it all perfect first. If we do, we will have failed, which is what we take up next, after our chapter exercise.

SHOW UP | ENGAGE | DO THE WORK

Take some time to answer the following:

1. What things scare or intimidate you the most?

2. What things have you always wanted to try or accomplish but have been too afraid to pursue?

3. What things are you avoiding because they make you uncomfortable?

4. What activities have you been meaning to pursue but need more courage to start?

5. What beliefs or assumptions are holding you back?

6. How can you take small, manageable steps toward your goals rather than trying to make a giant leap?

7. What are the benefits of taking action and stepping out of your comfort zone? How will doing so improve your life in the long run?

CHAPTER 7

Failure Is an Option

"There is no doubt in my mind that there are many ways to be a winner, but there is really only one way to be a loser, and that is to fail and not look beyond the failure."

— Kyle Rote Jr.

LEGEND HAS IT that in the 15th century, a Japanese shogun warrior treasured an ornate teacup that he somehow broke or fractured, prompting him to send it to China for repair. The shogun believed the masters there could restore the cup to its original form. After some time, the cup returned, held together by unsightly and impractical metal staples. Not only was it useless, but it was also ugly to boot.

Disappointed, the shogun sought out his own people to find a way to repair the cup. At the time, Japanese craftsmen commonly used a type of sticky tree sap as a lacquer to glue things together, so one of them came up with an idea. Why not use the lacquer to rejoin the cup's broken pieces, fill in its cracks, and mix it with gold dust to make it more aesthetically pleasing?

So, that's what they did.

As it turned out, the refurbished cup was returned in a more exquisite condition than its original form — revitalized with a new look and a second life.

And with that, *kintsugi*, or "golden repair," was born.

Since then, kintsugi has been a popular way to fix cracked and broken pottery and ceramics. Especially ones of value. More than just bonding the breaks and fractures with a camouflaging sealant, kintsugi celebrates each piece's one-of-a-kind history by highlighting its "scars." It's an inventive way to appreciate the beauty in imperfections and bring life to what has been broken.

And when we speak of things broken, a place to start is with Failure.

WHAT'S THIS THING CALLED FAILURE?

Failure has a bad connotation. Used to describe a wide range of experiences — from risky efforts that didn't pan out to traumatic losses — failure can feel devastating, like something that can't be undone or redone. It can paralyze us, depress us, and even limit our prospects of success moving forward.

Failure has a direct bearing on your outlook. It's demoralizing and unsettling, and it plays mind games with you. For instance, researchers from Purdue University conducted a study of the effects of failure on goal attainment.[39] In the study, random volunteers kicked an uncontested 20-yard field goal through goalposts directly in front of them. Researchers then interviewed the participants to see how they viewed their prospects of success on subsequent kicks.

Those who missed the kick on their first try were consistently found to view the goalposts as much higher and further away than those who were successful with their original kicks. Failure distorted the perception of the target, making it seem more unattainable.

In other studies, researchers found that when you fail, you are more likely to judge your skills and capabilities as significantly weaker than they are. For example, you develop a self-critical belief that you just don't have what it takes, experiencing negative feelings of guilt, shame, embarrassment, and self-blame.

You are at risk of creating a self-perpetuating cycle of fear and are more tempted to quit and give up. So much depends on how you look at these negative feelings: as a Fail or as a Failure.

Fail vs. Failure

There's a difference between Fail and Failure, just like there's a difference between guilt and shame.

> There's a difference between Fail and Failure, just like there's a difference between guilt and shame.

With guilt, you focus on unacceptable actions; you feel guilt when you do something wrong. Shame is an assessment of self; you feel shame when believing you are the type of person who is able to do the wrong.

Guilt is, "I did something bad." Shame is, "I am bad."

Similarly, fail says, "I made a mistake." Failure says, "I am a mistake." That's the difference.

This was certainly the case for my client, Stewart.

When I first met Stewart, he and several colleagues were deep in the trenches of a start-up that purchased prime residential properties for short-term vacation rental, similar to Airbnb or VRBO. Like many start-ups, the company ran into adversity and ultimately had to shut down. Stewart had poured much of his waking energy into the venture, not leaving much left over for his wife and young child.

When he approached me for coaching, Stewart struggled with self-doubt and shame. The collapse had a direct negative impact on his mindset. The venture hadn't just failed; he was a failure. I worked with Stewart on being able to say, "I'm not a failure. I simply failed in the venture." He saw that risk and failure are opposite sides of the same coin.

At the Risk of Failure

Stewart's story is not unique. A well-known statistic is that 9 out of 10 start-ups fail. 9 out of 10! Translation: To do big things requires taking big gambles… to take risks.

Remember: Everyone dies. Not everyone really lives. But when you live, you risk failing. That is, unless you live so cautiously that you might as well not have lived at all. In that case, you fail by default.

As author and speaker John Eldredge has put it, risk "requires something of us. It puts us to the test. We want to be tested, to discover we have what it takes."

Want to master a new skill? Prepare for the insecurity of being a beginner, where blunders are often unavoidable, and "dumb" questions are the only way forward.

Want to live life to its fullest? Get out of your comfort zone and dare.

Daring is not saying, "I'm willing to risk failure." Daring says, "I know I may eventually fail, and I'm still all in."

You do get fired. You do experience breakups. You do find yourself on the short end of the entrepreneurial stick. But you also miss 100 percent of shots you don't take. If you're not trying enough things that may lead to failure, you may not experience some remarkable breakthroughs in life that you hope to experience.

The key is what you discover when you risk; what you learn when you fail.

The key is what you discover when you risk; what you learn when you fail.

When you see Failure as a learning opportunity and look at it objectively (it's not personal), you will not fear it so much. So, it's the learning part of Failure that we turn next. But to do so, I want to take you back to that elementary school math competition I wrote about in Chapter 1.

FAILURE SUCKS BUT INSTRUCTS

Picture yourself back in school, standing at the chalkboard when the teacher calls out the following math problem: Minus 12 squared.

Immediately, your brain gets to work.

The first thing you remember is that when you square a number, it's the number multiplied by itself. In this case, it's 12 times 12. More importantly, you recall that when a negative is multiplied by a negative, the result is a positive.

The correct answer is 144 — not negative 144, but positive 144 — as crazy as that seems.

So now to the Delta Theorem.

Negative x Negative = Positive

As we just explored, we tend to view Failure as a setback, a devastation, a blow — all negatives. Using the same construct from math you turn negatives into positives when you "square up" your Failures You learn from them.

The key is to get past the blow, understand what happened and why it happened, and decide what to do differently next time. You redefine Failure by learning from it.

As John Maxwell, in his book, *Failing Forward*, put it, "Get a new definition of failure. Regard it as the price you pay for progress If you can do that, you will put yourself in a much better position to fail forward."

"Squaring up" Failure (f^2) is how we redefine it. And failing forward is the result.

Fail Forward Fast

Failing forward means that you purposefully and deliberately use Failure to move ahead. The basic idea is that as soon as possible after you make an effort, you think about what went right, what went wrong, and what could be done better next time.

You develop a "learning readiness." You don't dwell on Failure but find the time to think about it, analyze it, and move on.

Speed, it turns out, is a crucial variable. The faster you try again the better your chances of succeeding. However, the more time between attempts, the more likely you will fail again. That's why you fail forward fast.

In a broad study done on early career setbacks and future career impact, researchers found that "try and try again" only works if you learn from your previous Failures. According to Yang Wang from the Kellogg School of Management at Northwestern University, "You have to figure out what worked and what didn't and then focus on what needs to be improved instead of thrashing around and changing everything."

In other words, it pays to work smart, not hard. That was certainly the case for A.G. Lafley, the former CEO of Procter & Gamble.

In an interview with the Harvard Business Review, Lafley spoke about the process of learning from Failure when it came to building a successful corporate strategy.

Lafley and his team covered two kinds of learning: experience, which is gained from our own mistakes, and wisdom, which is learned from the mistakes of others.

Here's how he put it in the interview[40]:

> Many CEOs — including me — use innovation and acquisition to grow organically and inorganically in a balanced and sustained way. Both innovation and acquisition are risky and have high failure rates: 80 percent-plus for new product innovation in our industry; 70 percent-plus for acquisition. So, I had a team at P&G do a detailed analysis of all our acquisitions from 1970 to 2000. And the sobering story was that only 25 to 30 percent succeeded in that period. We studied the failures in detail. We pinpointed the problems and discovered patterns in our mistakes.

He went on to discuss the results of their efforts:

> Once we had identified the problems, we focused on what we had to change. How should we organize each phase of the acquisition? What processes should we put in place? What interim measures would tell us whether we were on track or off track? It's just a disciplined

> process, and you put somebody in charge of each phase of the process. Knowing what went wrong from 1970 to 2000, we were able to shift our acquisition success rate from below 30 percent to above 60 percent over the past 10 years. The whole idea of really studying, really going to school on failures, is so important. Because failures aren't the opposite of success. Failure is, in my view, all about learning. It's about learning what you can do better.

The evidence is clear. Failure is a powerful force for improvement when you learn from it.

WINNERS OFTEN BEGIN AS LOSERS

How many times do competitors have to lose before they win? Too many, most of them would say. So, we tend to see the wins, not the losses.

But it's often in the strain of loss… the strain of failing… where victory begins.

It's the fighter who has been knocked around previously that can go into a fight confident in the chances of winning. They know the darkness before dawn. They have a true and accurate sense of what winning will require them to do.

That sense is only possible because of the hard times — the hard knocks — they've experienced before. They have failed but learned from Failure.

Take Michael Jordan, arguably the greatest basketball player to have ever played the game. Here's what he had to say when talking about his Fails: "I've missed more than 9,000 shots in my career. I've lost almost 300 games. 26 times, I've been trusted to take the game-winning shot and missed. I've failed over and over and over again in my life. And that is why I succeed.'"[41]

It's Nietzsche's classic phrase, "what doesn't kill me makes me stronger," where paragons of grit and perseverance are forged.

But while coming back from Failure certainly teaches grit and perseverance, it turns out that's not what matters most. What matters most is how you respond to Failure and where that response leads.

For instance, studies have shown that after you have succeeded or failed, you learn the most when you think about what went wrong.

Learning from success alone is difficult because success does not create an urgent need to change. Instead, it reinforces what you already do and know. You succeeded. What more do you need?

With Failure, however, you have nothing available except to learn the valuable lessons offered.

I love how Stanford d.school founder David Kelley puts it: "If you keep making the same mistakes again and again, you aren't learning anything. If you keep making new and different mistakes, that means you are doing new things and learning new things." (And, I might add, really living.)

TYPES OF FAILURE

When I break down the way we fail, I have simplified it into two categories: Tooth-Suckers and SINKs.

Tooth-Suckers

Let's face it; some Failures are simply out of your control. Usually, these occur when you're dealing with complicated and complex circumstances. You do everything you can to put yourself in the best position to succeed, but you still run into a setback. A collapse happens that you didn't see coming because there was simply no way to see it coming. It merely happened because life is volatile, uncertain, chaotic, and ambiguous (VUCA).

Or you are trying something new and experimental. You are operating in "trial and error" mode and end up "trying and failing." You are innovating and exploring to grow your knowledge or expand your perspective, but things don't pan out.

I call these types of Failures "Tooth-Suckers."

Think of the times when you see someone run into some simple bad luck. Through no fault of their own, things simply turn against them, and they experience a setback.

When I see or read about these types of Failures, I find myself opening my lips just slightly, gritting my teeth, and then sucking in some air while making a bit of a ttttttsssssssssssssssss! sound going in. Then I purse my lips and murmur, "Ooooooohhh!" with a bit of empathetic pain in my tone.

It's a tooth-sucker, the recognition that you feel terrible for the other person because you can almost feel the pain of their misfortune.

There is not much you can do with a Tooth-Sucker Failure other than to recognize that sometimes stuff just happens. So, the only thing to do is to accept it, persevere through it, try to learn from it, and move on.

SINKs

SINKs are an entirely different story. SINKs are Failures that could have been, or should have been, foreseen but weren't. Or the types of Failures where you are too gripped by fear to take action, and you miss out as a result. This is the worst kind of Failure because, to a great extent, it is preventable.

I call them SINKs for a reason. There is a very sensitive part of the male anatomy that, when hit, causes extreme pain. Called by a slang term that is also the label for foods like almonds, pistachios, and cashews, this sensitive part resides in the groin area.

A SINK, then, is the acronym for a Self-Inflicted Nut Kick. (Apologies if this seems vulgar, but it really is an appropriate term for this type of Failure.) While the analogy focuses on the male anatomy, the concept of a SINK applies to men and women alike.

With a SINK, you realize that you likely could have prevented or avoided a Failure, but because you didn't prepare, plan, or take action as a result of being lazy, entitled, or even reluctant to listen to others, you failed. It is a self-inflicted Failure, the worst kind.

Remember, life is tough. It's even tougher if you're stupid. SINKs prove the point. And so have I.

Several years ago, I experienced an epic SINK that I am not proud of. I had just started a new position with a firm whereby I officed in a city that was an hour's plane ride from my home and family. At the beginning of each work week, I would commute from home to the office, stay the week in a rented apartment, and then commute back home for the weekend.

On this particular Friday, the firm held an office-wide gathering for all employees, complete with a wide assortment of food and libations. Being the new executive on the team, I was doing my best to get on the good side with my colleagues.

Unfortunately, I did a little "too good" of a job, to the point that when I tried to board my plane back home, the gate crew didn't think I was fit to board. Instead, they asked airport security to escort me to a local holding cell where I could become "fitter" to fly later. Needless to say, I missed my flight.

But that was not the worst of it.

Waiting for me at the airport back home were my wife and daughter. When I did not arrive on my scheduled flight, and they didn't hear a word from me (I was not allowed to make any calls), they freaked.

I won't go into more details about what happened beyond this other than to say it was an epic SINK on my behalf. Preventable. Avoidable. Stupid.

Why do I share such an embarrassing story? Because even as epic a Failure as it was — quite possibly as epic as it gets, in the worst kind of way — it forced me to practice what I preached. It caused me to take a deep look at everything that led up to my decisions, to learn from my mistake, and ultimately to humble myself and seek forgiveness from those I had hurt.

I had to "square up" my Failure.

Fortunately, there are other ways to prevent and learn from Failure than experiencing it, as I did with my SINK. There is a way to be proactive, which is where we turn next.

BE AWARE OF DISTORTIONS

We all like to believe that our decisions are rational and logical. When we take action, we are fully aware of all the factors necessary to make good choices, and we weigh the factors evenly.

If only that were true.

Instead, we are constantly influenced by subtle cognitive biases that, unless we are aware, can impact our better judgment. And when better judgment is impacted, often SINKs are lurking not far away.

Awareness of common biases can put you in a better position to avoid and possibly prevent SINKs.

Here is a list of some of the more common cognitive biases:

- **Confirmation bias** – this is the tendency to search out, favor, recall, and interpret information in a way that confirms or supports what you believe or what you want to believe. It can make early successes look better than they are or cause you to disregard things that happen as not relevant because they don't fit with what you want. It's the easiest of biases to fall into because it supports what you desire to have happen rather than being open to whatever might happen.

- **Overoptimism bias** — closely associated with confirmation bias, this is the tendency to be overconfident in future prospects while underestimating future challenges. While optimism is a driving force behind things like Passion, overoptimism interferes with proper planning and design. Overoptimism can also cause you to miss fatal flaws or opportunities to pivot and change direction in a timely manner.
- **False-consensus bias** – this is the tendency to see your own choices and judgments as relatively common and appropriate to existing circumstances. It can compound problems created by other biases, causing you to head down paths you don't want to go.
- **Availability bias** – this is the tendency to believe that examples that come easily to your mind are more commonplace than they are. For instance, you might be fooled into thinking that your unsatisfied needs are more common than they are.

These are but a few of the many, many biases that are out there. My point in bringing them up is not to put disproportionate emphasis on any one of these biases but rather to point out that awareness of bias can go a long way toward preventing Failure from happening.

Yes, it's valuable to learn from our mistakes, but it's preferable to avoid them in the first place.

There's one more area we need to cover when speaking of "squaring up" Failure. It might be the most crucial area of all.

BEWARE THE VOWS YOU MAKE

Not all learning is good for us. There are many times when what you learn is downright destructive.

For instance, if the lessons you learn from Failure are just flat wrong or from a source that proves unreliable, you can find yourself in an even deeper hole than you thought possible. So, using discernment with what you learn is critical.

One good way is to review your Principles to see how things line up. For example, did you do anything that would violate the things you hold to be true?

Another is to tap into the wisdom of others to help assess things that went wrong. For example, do you have people you can run things past in your life?

But the most important thing you must do is to avoid making a negative personal pledge after experiencing Failure. Here's what I mean:

How many times, after having experienced Failure, have you found yourself saying, "I will **NEVER** (*fill in the blank*) again!"

You embarrassingly cry when tagged out at home plate and say, "I will **NEVER** be wimpy again!"

You panic when put on the spot and say, "I will **NEVER** speak up in a meeting again!"

You experience a romantic breakup and say, "I will **NEVER** put my heart out there again!"

We make vows with ourselves to never risk, never try, and never live again.

Beware the lessons you choose to embrace when you fail. They may not be true. Once you buy into them, you come under the sway of that particular interpretation of Failure. And then you make a personal vow. It then often plays itself out; it becomes self-fulfilling. And when it does, you may find yourself having inadvertently vowed to, as Emerson put it, live a life of quiet desperation.

OK, let's close this chapter with some of the best thoughts I've heard regarding Failure.

ENDING WHERE WE STARTED

In 2008, *Harry Potter* author J. K. Rowling was asked to give a Commencement Address at Harvard University. As she addressed the graduates on their futures, she spoke of the benefits of failure[42]:

> So, why do I talk about the benefits of failure? Simply because failure meant a stripping away of the inessential. I stopped pretending to myself that I was anything other than what I was and began to direct all my energy into finishing the only work that mattered to me. Had I really succeeded at anything else, I might never have found the determination to succeed in the one arena I believed I truly belonged. I was set free because my greatest fear had been realized, and I was still alive, and I still had a daughter whom I adored, and I had an old typewriter and a big idea. And so rock bottom became the solid foundation on which I rebuilt my life.

Rowling went on to share what she had learned from failing:

> Failure gave me an inner security that I had never attained by passing examinations. Failure taught me things about myself that I could have learned no other

> way. I discovered that I had a strong will, and more discipline than I had suspected; I also found out that I had friends whose value was truly above the price of rubies.

Your mistakes, failures, fractures, and breaks are opportunities to create something even more beautiful than before. Sometimes in repairing things that have broken… in applying kintsugi in your own life… you create something more unique, radiant, and resilient.

J. K. Rowling did. So can you.

SHOW UP | ENGAGE | DO THE WORK

Take some time to answer the following:

1. Analyze a recent Failure. What caused it? Was it a lack of planning, poor execution, or another factor?

2. What can be learned from the Failure? What can be done differently in the future to avoid similar Failures?

3. What were the consequences of the Failure?

4. What was the impact on your reputation? Your credibility?

5. What actions can be taken to prevent similar Failures in the future? What changes can be made to processes, systems, or practices to improve outcomes and reduce the risk of Failure?

6. What can be done to recover from the Failure?

7. How can the lessons learned from this Failure be shared with others?

CHAPTER 8

Making a Difference

"We gon shock the world."

— Juwan Howard

I RECENTLY CAME across a son's obituary — written for all the world to see — of his recently deceased father. It disturbed me. I'm guessing it will disturb you as well. When I first read it, I thought it might be some comic sketch. A meme. It's not. It is, in fact, an actual obituary.

The obituary opens like this:

> *He was born in Belmont, NY, on April 16, 1941. He passed away on June 27, 2022, living a long life, much longer than he deserved. He is survived by his three children, no four. Oops, five children. Well as of 2022 we believe there is one more that we know about, but there could be more. His love was abundant when it came to himself, but for his children it was limited.*

> *From a young age, he was a ladies' man and an abusive alcoholic, solidifying his commitment to both with the path of destruction he left behind, damaging his adult children, and leaving them broken.*[43]

Never have I read such a raw and public account of pain and anger caused by a life not well-lived. But perhaps the most disturbing of al was the way it ended. "His passing proves that evil does eventually die, and it marks a time of healing, which will allow his children to ge the closure they deserve. He can be remembered for being a father tc many, and a dad to none."

Yikes!

Now contrast that with another obituary I read about another father to many, only this the father of an entire nation. It starts like this

> *He was born in the small town of Porbandar on October 2, 1869. He belonged by birth to the Vaishya, or trading caste. His father died when he was 15 years old, and from that time, his mother became the greatest influence in his life. When 19, he came to London, qualified as a barrister, and returning to Bombay in 1892, set up in practice. In 1896 he went to the Transvaal to help a client in a legal suit. That visit changed the whole course of his life. Seeing the social and political disabilities of his fellow countrymen, he decided to help them, and soon became their political leader and adviser. He went on steadily preparing his followers for the struggle which was to end the indignities under which they struggled.*[44]

What a difference. Though each lived in different eras, each left marks on their worlds. The first, a mark that left wounds that only his death healed. The second, a mark that healed the wounds of an entire people... and whose life is a prime example of the concept of Delta as used in the Delta Theorem.

That second man was Mahatma Gandhi.

BE THE CHANGE

Through his philosophy of nonviolent resistance for social change, Mahatma Gandhi believed in the power of individuals to make a difference in the world through their actions and example. He was not only an important figure in India's struggle for independence from British rule, but to this day, he remains one of the most influential figures the world has ever seen. One of his most influential quotes, "Be the change that you wish to see in the world," perfectly embodies the concept of Delta in the Delta Theorem.

It also set me on an exploratory quest to see what part the elements of the Theorem, if any, might have played in activating it in his own life. Call it a case study of sorts. Reverse engineering to see if and how the various elements of the Theorem... Purpose, Priorities, Principles, Passion, Effort, Failure... played a part in the life of such a great man.

Here's what I discovered:

Priorities: Gandhi understood that independence and the right to govern oneself were essential for human flourishing and development. He understood that the welfare of the individual was connected to the welfare of the community. So, it's clear from his story that he set working for independence, self-government, and betterment as top Priorities in his life.

Principles: Clearly, Principles played an important role in Gandhi's life. He consistently maintained that violence was never justified; that it was important to seek change through nonviolent means, despite experiencing violence throughout his life. He held that truth was the most potent force for change, and holding firm to one's Principles, even in the face of opposition, was the most important virtue one can hold.

Passion: No doubt, Gandhi had Passion. His zeal toward mobilizing and inspiring his followers for the cause of independence through civil disobedience and peaceful resistance was legendary, even in the face of opposition that targeted him for assassination attempts, arrests, and imprisonments. He vigorously encouraged followers to think beyond their interests and strive for the elevation of the entire society.

Alpha (Purpose): Gandhi had a primary focus: seeking independence from British rule. It was a powerful WHY set above all else. It's no wonder. When connecting what he saw as most important (self-government, betterment of all) with the non-negotiables upon which he took his stands (nonviolence, truth) and a fire that burned inside (mobilizing followers, selflessness), Gandhi's purpose easily followed. Independence was his ikigai, his reason for being.

Effort: Gandhi worked tirelessly to mobilize his followers and himself for the cause of independence. For instance, in response to the British government's decision to impose sweeping powers to suppress political opposition and jail political activists without trial, Gandhi launched the Non-Cooperation Movement, calling on Indians to boycott British goods and institutions. Later, in defiance of the government's monopoly on salt production, Gandhi led a protest against the British government's salt tax, joining with his followers on a 24-day, 240-mile march to the sea. In other words, Gandhi did not just talk about independence; he took action. It's doubtful independence would have ever come during his lifetime absent taking action.

Failure: In 1922, a group of Gandhi's followers attacked and killed several police officers, striking a massive setback for Gandhi. He saw the incident as a Failure on his part to educate and discipline the protesters adequately, and he concluded that the Indian people were not yet ready for the type of mass civil disobedience that he had envisioned. As a result, Gandhi called off the Non-Cooperation Movement and, having learned from the Failure, later shifted his focus to more local, decentralized forms of resistance and community-building.

Delta: Through his leadership, Gandhi was able to mobilize millions of Indians to peacefully resist British rule, leading to the withdrawal of British forces from India and the creation of the independent nation. His teachings and methods of peaceful protest have inspired civil rights and freedom movements, including the Civil Rights Movement led by Martin Luther King, Jr. Gandhi's life and work continue to be a source of inspiration and influence for people around the world.

So, am I saying that Gandhi's life is a proof of the Delta Theorem? No. I am saying that when I researched common elements found in the lives of those who are difference makers, just as with Gandhi, I found undeniable evidence that the elements of the Theorem played a significant role in making a Difference.

OK. Let me shift gears a bit here.

I realize it's easy to be intimidated when looking at a life like Gandhi's. As if in some way, he and others like him — the Abraham Lincolns, the Harriett Tubmans, the Nelson Mandelas — are somehow superhuman, always knowing exactly what to do, and able to do it, regardless of circumstances or challenges. "I can never be a Gandhi," we think, so we make it too easy to dismiss holding him up as realistic for being a difference maker.

And likewise, it's easy to feel that one person can't make a difference. The world has so many big problems that often seem impossible to solve. And making a difference isn't always instant, nor is it necessarily large-scale. It can take months, even years, as was the case for Gandhi. But making the world a better place often means bettering it for a few people at a time.

So, what if, instead of trying to be some invincible force, we tried to be a little bit better whenever we saw an opportunity? What kind of cumulative difference would that end up making?

Every action has an impact, no matter how small. It may seem insignificant, but the ripple effect of a kind act can be far-reaching and profound. We can be inspired by the likes of Gandhi, Lincoln, Tubman, and Mandela to use our actions to create positive change. Instead of feeling overwhelmed by the enormity of the task, we can focus on making a difference in our own corner of the world. By taking small steps and making small changes, we can work toward creating a larger impact in the long run, similar to a butterfly's effect in making a difference with the weather.

Every action has an impact, no matter how small. It may seem insignificant, but the ripple effect of a kind act can be far-reaching and profound.

BUTTERFLY EFFECT

I've always been somewhat perplexed by meteorologists. You know, those folks who have their own segment on every newscast, telling us what we need to wear going out, sometimes seven to ten days in advance. It's the only job I know where you are paid to give advice that deeply affects everyday lives, yet you're never held accountable. (OK, maybe meteorologists and Wall Street talking heads, who seem to make predictions on the financial markets all the time but are never checked after the fact.) Yet, despite the lack of accountability, I still find myself turning to the meteorologist for advice on what to wear, though I usually double-check their forecasts with a few other sources to make sure I am prepared for whatever Mother Nature might throw at me.

One of the more interesting concepts that has its genesis from these modern "Nostradomai" (my plural for Nostradamus) is a concept known as the Butterfly Effect. The Butterfly Effect describes how small, seemingly insignificant actions can have far-reaching and sometimes unforeseen consequences. It's named after the metaphor of a butterfly flapping its wings in one part of the world, causing a tornado to occur in another part of the world.

For example, imagine a Monarch butterfly flapping its wings in South Africa. I don't honestly know if Monarch butterflies even exist in South Africa, but let's assume they do. The idea is that this minuscule activity — the flapping of the wings in, say, central South Africa — has a rippling effect that causes a breeze to occur over the Cape Town coastline, which then causes wind gusts over the South Atlantic, which gains momentum off the coast of Brazil, altering the path of a hurricane formed in the Caribbean, and causing it to make landfall in Nicaragua as opposed to Cuba as initially predicted. In other words, this small change in air currents caused by a butterfly flapping its wings could have a major impact on the path of a hurricane and the communities it affects.

The idea is that, in a complex and interconnected system, even the slightest shift can make an enormous difference. Above and behind and beyond the sometimes-confusing chaos, something is going on here. Small changes can cause a chain reaction, leading to very different results. From a butterfly flapping its wings to an ocean current to a swirling hurricane, there's a logic, a meaning, an unfolding pattern.

In other words, big actions take place in the little actions of life. Every time you change just one person's world, you're starting a Butterfly Effect with the potential to improve lives for generations to come. I have certainly seen this in the lives of many people I have coached, advised, or worked with over the years.

Here are but a few that stand out in what I like to call a "Delta Force"

Lorraine Gary Sheinberg (actress, filmmaker, and human rights activist): Unless you are familiar with the business of Hollywood, you may not know the name Sheinberg. If you are, you'll recognize Sid Sheinberg as synonymous with all things Hollywood. With integrity. And with Steven Spielberg.

You'll also know that the force behind the force of Sid Sheinberg has always been Lorraine Gary Sheinberg, his wife of over 60 years before his passing and my long-time client.

Best known for her role as Sheriff Brody's spouse Ellen in the film *Jaws*, Lorraine's acting career spanned several decades. Self-deprecating in an ever-endearing way, Lorraine was once on record saying, "I've been a brilliant failure." Nothing could be further from the truth. Her passionate advocacy of social causes — spreading awareness about AIDS, women's empowerment, and education for girls — has made a lasting difference around the globe.

Her deep Principles have been a driving force in her humanitarian efforts — efforts such as producing and directing *Shroud of Silence: Gender Apartheid in Afghanistan*, an award-winning short documentary chronicling the everyday struggle of Afghan women and girls under the Taliban regime's brutal system of gender apartheid. The documentary drew huge awareness to the plight of Afghan women even before 9/11, making a huge difference not just in Afghanistan but around the globe.

And while those are facts about Lorraine, here's why she's the real deal in making a difference: In all my years advising her and Sid, I have never experienced anyone as committed to causes as she. And consistent in doing so. We don't see eye-to-eye on our worldviews, but one thing I always know about Lorraine is where she stands.

And even in our disagreements, she shows respect. I am a better man as a result.

Rob Francais (CEO of Aspiriant): In 2008, Rob Francais co-founded Aspiriant, now one of the fastest-growing wealth management firms in the country. In 2012, I was fortunate to have joined forces with him at the firm.

Like many visionary CEOs, Rob has an uncanny ability to see a different future and get others to see it as well. In the case of Aspiriant, Rob's "city on a hill" is to do something that has yet to be done, make a difference in an industry that has been around for hundreds of years by building the first national, independent, and objective wealth management firm. One with a culture and way of doing business that durably aligns clients' interests with the interests of those he is leading.

But it's more than being a difference maker in an industry where Rob has set his sights. It's in making a difference in the lives of those he leads. "I love making a difference for the two communities we serve: our clients and our people," he has said. And he's good at it.

I know. I was one of his people.

So those are the facts about Rob. Here's why he's the real deal in making a difference: Rob brings a blue-collar mindset into a white-collar world. As a kid, he sold T-shirts at swap meets and doesn't shy away from telling about it. He's authentic. He makes everyone in his organization feel like they are important. Because they are.

And it's not for show. It's with purpose, on purpose.

Mark Divine (author, podcaster, and retired Navy SEAI Commander): The highest ranked trainee of his SEAL BUD/S class Mark Divine served nine years on active duty and 11 as a reserve retiring as a commander. In his service career, he led teams so effec tively that the U.S. government engaged him to develop a nationwid mentoring program for SEAL trainees. Eventually, he adapted it t train non-SEALs as well, including me.

Driven by a Passion for transforming lives, Mark has a powerfu vision: Train 100 million people to lead with courage and compassion make transformational learning and coaching accessible to anyone and help veterans and first responders find their purpose. Having bee certified under his Unbeatable Mind certification program, somethin I wrote about earlier in the book, I am one of the 100 million.

"All individuals are not only capable of and deeply driven to b better and do better," he has said. "Many just don't have the tools."

Again, those are the facts about Mark. Here's why he's the real dea when it comes to making a difference: Mark eats his own cooking. Hi foundation, The Courage Foundation, runs an annual Burpees for Vet fundraiser. At 59, Mark is there doing burpees with everyone else. H constantly ups his thought leadership game, pushing those around hin to up theirs. He has expanded the SEAL ethos and made all of us fee we, too, are part of the Teams.

Kimberly Inskeep (CEO of cabi): While being voted "Bes Dressed" by her high school senior class, Kimberly Inskeep neve could have guessed she'd end up spearheading a $250 million fashio business. Instrumental in the development and launch of a women' clothing line and innovative retail sales model that spurned brick an mortar way before everyone else was doing it, Kimberly founded th cabi Fashion Experience believing there was a better way for wome to both shop and work, especially given the demands on women's lives

"We never wanted to be a business seeking to be successful for success' sake, but as a way for us to do good for others," Kimberly has said. "From the inception, we knew this business would only be worthwhile for us if we created a lasting impact on the lives of women, and we dreamed that would also include women all over the world."

As a personal friend who sat at her dinner table when cabi started out of her garage, and having watched its explosive growth since, I have witnessed the difference her tireless efforts have made in women's lives.

And once again, those are the facts about Kimberly. Here's why she's the real deal when it comes to making a difference: Kimberly, along with her husband, Jim, give generously of their time, talent, and treasure. From supporting causes financially to opening her home for gatherings, she uses her success to raise the tide for others, making us feel special.

As Lorraine, Rob, Mark, and Kimberly show, you don't have to be a Mahatma Gandhi, or an Abraham Lincoln, or a Harriett Beecher Stowe to make a difference. Each of them knows their Priorities, stands on Principles, pursues a Passion, understands their purpose, makes a huge Effort, and has learned from Failure. Each has taken to heart this poem by Edward Everett Hale[45]:

> I am only one,
> But still I am one.
> I cannot do everything,
> But still I can do something;
> And because I cannot do everything,
> I will not refuse to do something that I can do.

But they all have something even more. Each, in their own way and sphere of influence, senses something larger than themselves is going on. They appreciate that though each of their individual stories feels large, a much larger story is going on. One that we're all caught up in.

THE LARGER STORY

Several years ago, a colleague introduced me to the work of Franciscan friar and author Richard Rohr. It literally changed my life.

In one of his most penetrating insights, Rohr describes how wholehearted people live within at least three levels of meaning: "My Story," "Our Story," and "The Story."

My Story: According to Rohr, "My Story" comprises our private lives: all the unique things where we proudly proclaim, "This is me!" It's the level where we perform on our own small stage. Where the questions are, "Who is watching me? How do I feel? What do I believe? What makes me unique?" It's full of subjective, interpersonal, and self-help language. "My Story" is not big enough to create significant or meaningful designs, so it creates dramas, tragedies, and victimhood to put itself on a larger stage.

Our Story: "Our Story" is about us. It's our group, community, country — whatever pack that provides reasons for belonging, attaching, trusting, and loving. It's where we trumpet, "This is us!" Rohr says it's where most live their lives: identifying entirely with their ethnicity, their gender, their group, their religion, and their occupations. There is true comfort in being among our own. Unfortunately, so many spend their lives defending the group's borders and "glory," and we end up with culture and identity wars.

The Story: Rohr describes the most expansive level of meaning as "The Story," the domain of universal understanding that holds "My Story" and

"Our Story" together. The way we move to "The Story" is to take responsibility for both our personal story and our group story. Those who live in "The Story" look at the smaller stage with eyes like two full moons because they can see the much larger story we're all caught up in. When we are connected to "The Story" and not just "My Story" or "Our Story," we are now connected to something wide-ranging and limitless. Our gladness meets the world's need.

When we are connected to "The Story" and not just "My Story" or "Our Story," we are now connected to something wide-ranging and limitless. Our gladness meets the world's need.

The concept is similar to a Russian Matryoshka doll, those wooden dolls of increasing size found one inside the other. The largest of the dolls that encompasses the other two is "The Story." As you open up "The Story," you discover "Our Story." Then, as you open up "Our Story," you find "My Story."

While “My Story” or “Our Story” may feel quite large — spouse
kids, pets, jobs, houses, cars, bank accounts, investments — there is
much larger story that we are all caught up in. It’s “The Story.”

That, in essence, is what the Delta Theorem is all about — mak
ing a difference in the world at any scale, from a local community t
the global level. It involves advancing important causes or issues o
contributing to a particular field or discipline. It also involves inspir
ing and motivating others to pursue their own goals and dreams. I
requires dedication, hard work, and a willingness to take risks an
push boundaries.

And in the end, when we do, I guarantee we will be fully alive..
and truly wealthy.

SHOW UP | ENGAGE | DO THE WORK

Take some time to answer the following:

1. How can you make the most impact with your available time and resources?
2. What challenges or obstacles do you anticipate in trying to make a difference? How can you overcome them?
3. How can you measure the impact of your efforts?
4. How can you sustain your efforts over the long term?
5. How can you involve and empower others to make a difference?
6. How can you stay motivated and inspired to keep working toward positive change?

CHAPTER 9

Just One Chisel Away

THE ROMAN STOIC Hierocles spoke of "circles of concern" as concentric rings that work outward, starting with our minds, then moving to our bodies, our families, our communities, our cities, our countries, our empires, and our world. The work, he said, was to draw this outer concern inward, to learn how to care as much as possible for as many people as possible, to do as much good for them as possible.

Hierocles' philosophy is incredibly relevant today as our world is more interconnected than ever. We can feel the impact of our actions and decisions on people and places around the world, and it's up to us to decide how much we can care for those outside our circles.

All of us have splendor and glory within us. To unveil it starts with recognizing our potential and then putting in the hard work needed to reveal that splendor and glory. With the right mindset, we can all create masterpieces that will stand the test of time.

Like the layout of Michelangelo's works in the Galleria dell'Accademia that I described at the beginning of this book, that's ultimately what the Delta Theorem is all about — a transformation from within, creating something beautiful and unique.

A coming alive with purpose, on purpose.

You've already taken the first step by reading this book. Now, it's time to Show Up, Engage, and Do the Work.

- Celebrate every single step of progress, no matter how big or small.
- Understand that setbacks are inevitable and that Failure is not only okay but necessary to learn and grow.
- And finally, recognize that no matter how hard it may seem the result will be worth the Effort.

Don't *Just Do It.* Just Do You.

In doing so, you will put yourself in the best position to be fully alive… and truly wealthy.

$$\frac{a}{p^3} \times \varepsilon f^2 = \Delta$$

Where a = powerful WHY
p^3 = Priorities · Principles · Passion
ε = Effort
f = Failure
Δ = Difference/Change/Impact

APPENDIX

Creating Rituals

CREATING RITUALS CAN be tricky because it requires us to think outside the box and come up with unique and meaningful ways to bring special moments and emotions into our lives. Faced with this creative challenge, I compiled a list of 100 different actions that could become part of a valuable ritual.

- Use a hopeful mantra
- Play an instrument
- Do karaoke
- Watch a play or concert
- Clean up a room or house
- Develop a hobby
- Paint or draw
- Be adventurous
- Be kind to people
- Smile more
- Share feelings
- Identify today's Priorities
- Plan the day
- Meditate
- Start a new project
- Make a to-do list
- Drink water
- Dance to music
- Attend a class
- Say no
- Bite your tongue
- Hug lover
- Take a break and relax
- Go for a run
- Walk the dog
- Focused uninterrupted hour
- Learn a new skill
- Get a massage
- Be present
- Pay bills
- Play a game
- Wake up early
- Express love

- Do the most difficult task first
- Update monthly goals
- Plan for next week
- Get up and stretch
- Play a favorite sport
- Unplug and be with self
- Watch a TED talk
- Track expenses
- Learn a new skill
- Develop passive income streams
- Be fully present
- Study something new
- Pray or meditate
- Focus on the positive
- Spend time in nature
- Connect with creator
- Host a family dinner
- Spend quality time with family
- Return items to their proper place
- Consult with a mentor or coach
- Review progress and adjust plan
- Take a long bath
- Go to sleep early
- Go for a bike ride
- Manage spending
- Write in journal
- Date with spouse
- Play with kids
- Send a love letter
- Review life goals
- Try a new experience
- Take a break every hour
- Attend religious service
- Travel to a new place
- Hang out with friends
- Arrange a family vacation
- Use time in traffic wisely
- Talk to a stranger
- Collaborate with colleagues
- Take a deep breath and relax
- Challenge self
- Pay off debt
- Eat vegetables or fruit
- Review saving plan
- Balance budget
- Read a book
- Listen to kids
- Compliment partner
- Invest in self
- Create or build something
- Focus on one thing at a time
- Gift, give, help someone
- Use a sauna or jacuzzi
- Reconnect with an old buddy
- Set up a sensual environment
- Contribute or volunteer
- Take a cold shower

- Recycle, repurpose, give away, or throw away one item
- Refuse to gripe, complain, or talk about anything negative
- Engage in prolonged eye contact
- Deliberately visualize something pleasant and calming
- Network or develop new relationships

Thank You

I WOULD LIKE to thank you, the reader, for your time and interest in this book. Your support and feedback are what make this all worthwhile. I am eager to hear about your thoughts and experiences as you delve into these pages. On Amazon or other sites, please share your feedback on how this book helped you. You can also follow me on Twitter at @bretmagpiong and check out the Rudius Strategies Group website at www.rudiusstrategiesgroup.com.

With heartfelt gratitude,
Bret Magpiong

About the Author

CERTIFIED COACH BRET Magpiong has served his entire professional career as both an advisor to entrepreneurs, executives, professional athletes, entertainers, and their respective companies and as a C-Level executive for various firms in the wealth management industry. Many of the individuals and companies he has advised and served have been recognized on the Forbes 400 and Fortune 500 listings.

Bret started his career at PriceWaterhouse long before they were known as PricewaterhouseCoopers and back when they were part of the so-called "Big 8" professional services firms. Clueless to this, while being recruited and asked what he knew about the "Big 8," he began by talking about a college football conference in the Midwest, an embarrassing fact that he attributes to having likely landed him the job.

He has been featured in *The Wall Street Journal*, the RIA Channel, the Family Wealth Alliance, and Schwab IMPACT. Notably, he once gave an acceptance speech at the *MovieGuide®* awards for his involvement with the movie *Millions*, but also, unfortunately, once promoted one of the lowest attended international soccer friendlies in the history of Chicago's Toyota Park. All of these experiences have contributed to his unique insight into personal growth and empowerment.

In addition to his professional accomplishments, Bret is an experienced athlete who has completed a SEALFit 20X and 20SX, a New York Marathon, GoRuck Tough, and Hermosa Beach Triathlon. He has been married to his wife, Leyla, for over 30 years, and they have one successfully launched daughter. They currently reside in California.

CONNECT WITH BRET

You can reach Bret through the following channels:

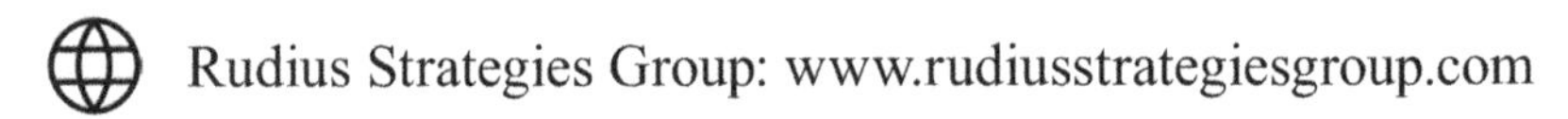
Rudius Strategies Group: www.rudiusstrategiesgroup.com

https://www.linkedin.com/in/bret-magpiong-ab9b2134/

@bretmagpiong

Endnotes

1 *Jerry Maguire*, directed by Cameron Crowe (1996; Culver City, CA: TriStar Pictures).
2 *The Godfather Part III*, directed by Francis Ford Coppola (1990; United States: Paramount Pictures).
3 *The Wizard of Oz*, directed by Victor Fleming (1939; United States: Metro-Goldwyn-Mayer).
4 *The Emperor's Club*, directed by Michael Hoffman (2002; United States: Universal Pictures).
5 Roy F. Baumeister, Catrin Finkenauer, Kathleen D. Vohs, "Bad is stronger than good," *Review of General Psychology*, 5, no. 4 (2001): 323–370, doi:10.1037/1089-2680.5.4.323. S2CID 13154992.
6 *Mad Max: Beyond Thunderdome*, directed by George Miller and George Ogilvie (1991; Kennedy Miller Productions, Warner Bros.).
7 Viktor E. Frankl, *The Will to Meaning: Foundations and Applications of Logotherapy*, New York: New American Library, 1970).
8 Merriam-Webster.com Dictionary, s.v. "commitment," accessed December 20, 2022, https://www.merriam-webster.com/dictionary/commitment.
9 Dwight D. Eisenhower, Address at the Second Assembly of the World Council of Churches, August 19, 1954, archived at https://web.archive.org/web/20150402111315/http:/www.presidency.ucsb.edu/ws/?pid=9991.

10 Taken from RadReads, "How to Prioritize (When Everything's a Priority)," accessed February 11, 2023, https://radreads.co/radical-prioritization/.

11 Friedrich Wilhelm Nietzsche, *Thus Spoke Zarathustra: a Book for All and None,* 1883.

12 Ryan Holiday, "The Earth Is Big and Has Room for Everyone," Daily Stoic, 2022, https://dailystoic.com/the-earth-is-big-and-has-room-for-everyone-2/.

13 *Animal House*, directed by John Landis (1978; Universal Pictures).

14 *City Slickers*, directed by Ron Underwood (1991; United States: Columbia Pictures, Metro-Goldwyn-Mayer).

15 David Brooks, *The Road to Character* (New York: Random House, 2016).

16 Dorothy Neufeld, "The World's Most Influential Values, In One Graphic," *Visual Capitalist*, November 5, 2020, https://www.visualcapitalist.com/most-influential-values/

17 Leidy Klotz, *Subtract: The Untapped Science of Less* (New York NY: Flatiron Books, 2021).

18 Ray Dalio, *Principles: Life and Work* (New York: Simon and Schuster, 2017).

19 Ray Dalio, *Principles: Life and Work*. (New York: Simon and Schuster).

20 Taken from DailyDad.com, "Setting Rules for Your Children: Why You Need Rules, Examples of Rules, How to Enforce Them, and More," accessed February 11, 2023, https://dailydad.com/rules-for-your-children/.

21 Victor Hugo, *Les Misérables* (Penguin Classics, 1982).

22 MJ Zawadzki, JM Smyth, and HJ Costigan, "Real-Time Associations Between Engaging in Leisure and Daily Health and Well-Being," *Ann Behav Med.*, 49, no. 4 (Aug 2015): 605-15, doi: 10.1007/s12160-015-9694-3. PMID: 25724635.

23 Interview with Wendy Kopp, “Leading an Educational Evolution,” Academy of Achievement, September 13, 2013, https://achievement.org/achiever/wendy-kopp/#interview.

24 John Eldredge, *The Journey of Desire: Searching for the Life You’ve Always Dreamed Of* (Thomas Nelson, 2016).

25 The Daily Stoic, Episode 38: “Love Always,” October 8, 2018, https://wondery.com/shows/the-daily-stoic/episode/11074-love-always/.

26 RJ Vallerand, C. Blanchard, GA Mageau, R. Koestner, C. Ratelle, M. Leonard M. Gagne, and J. Marsolais, “Les passions de l’ame: on obsessive and harmonious passion,” *J Pers Soc Psychol.* 85, no. 4 (Oct. 2003): 756-67, doi: 10.1037/0022-3514.85.4.756. PMID: 14561128.

27 Angela Duckworth, *Grit: The Power of Passion and Perseverance*, (New York, NY: Scribner, 2016).

28 Bill Plotkin, *Soulcraft: Crossing into the Mysteries of Nature and Psyche*, (Novato, Calif. New World Library).

29 Wilma A. Iggers, *Women of Prague: Ethnic Diversity and Social Change from the Eighteenth Century to the Present.* (Providence: Berghahn Books, 1995).

30 Pierre Pichère and Anne-Christine Cadiat, Maslow’s *Hierarchy of Needs*, (Namur: Lemaitre, 2015).

31 William Burnett and David J. Evans, *Designing Your Life: How to Build a Well-lived, Joyful Life*, (New York: Alfred A. Knopf, 2016).

32 Khe Hy, “The Magic of Doing $10,000 per Hour Work,” RadReads, 2022, https://radreads.co/10k-work/.

33 Tim Grover and Shari Lesser Wenk, *Relentless: From Good to Great to Unstoppable* (New York: Scribner, 2013).

34 Tim Grover and Shari Lesser Wenk, *Relentless*, 2013.

35 Lance P. Hickey, “‘Flow’ Experiences: The Secret to Ultimate Happiness?” *HuffPost*, November 17, 2011, https://www.huffpost.com/entry/flow-experiences-happiness_b_811682.

36 Brene Brown, *Rising Strong* (London, England: Vermilion, 2015).
37 George Kingsley Zipf, *Human Behavior and the Principle of Least Effort: An Introduction to Human Ecology* (Addison-Wesley Press, 1949).
38 M. Easter, *The Comfort Crisis: Embrace Discomfort to Reclaim Your Wild, Happy, Healthy Self* (United States: Potter/Ten Speed/Harmony/Rodale, 2021).
39 JK Witt and TE Dorsch, "Kicking to bigger uprights: field goal kicking performance influences perceived size, *Perception*, 38 no. 9 (2009): 1328-40, doi: 10.1068/p6325. PMID: 19911630.
40 Karen Dillon, "I Think of My Failures as a Gift," *Harvard Business Review*, April 2011, https://hbr.org/2011/04/i-think-of-my-failures-as-a-gift
41 Taken from a Nike commercial, viewable at https://www.youtube.com/watch?v=GuXZFQKKF7A&t=22s.
42 Taken from Text of J.K. Rowlings' Speech, *The Harvard Gazette* June 5, 2008, https://news.harvard.edu/gazette/story/2008/06/text-of-j-k-rowling-speech/.
43 Obituary, Lawrence Pfaff Sr., *Florida Times Union*, July 2, 2022, https://www.jacksonville.com/obituaries/pfla0245589.
44 *The Guardian*, "31 January 1948: Mahatma Gandhi Dies," accessed February 11, 2023, https://www.theguardian.com/theguardian/from-the-archive-blog/2011/may/27/guardian190-gandhi-obituary-1948.
45 The poem has been attributed to several different people throughout the years, including Hale, as well as Edwin Osgood Grover and Helen Keller.

UNITING PEOPLE THROUGH THE POWER OF STORIES

A motivating speaker can excite you about what you're already doing; inspiring thought leaders invigorate you to be the best version of yourself. They are the visionaries and dreamers whose stories bring life to the human spirit.

BRET MAGPIONG
is one of those visionaries and dreamers.

His compelling stories make you look at the big picture of your own life or the life of your organization, giving rise to the practical application of key ideas to your situation, in your own unique way.

Keynotes, Seminars, Podcasts, Workshops, Conferences, Retreats... Bret handles them all.

To book Bret, visit **www.rudiusstrategiesgroup.com.**

Made in the USA
Las Vegas, NV
12 May 2023